**PARTY COALITIONS
IN NIGERIA**

History, Trends and Prospects

PARTY COALITIONS IN NIGERIA
History, Trends and Prospects

Anthony A. Akinola

Safari Books Ltd
Ibadan

Published by
Safari Books Ltd
Ile Ori Detu
1, Shell Close
Onireke
Ibadan.
Email: safarinigeria@gmail.com

© Anthony A. Akinola

Publisher: Chief Joop Berkhout, *OON*
Deputy Publisher: George Berkhout

First Published 2014

All rights reserved. This book is copyright and so no part of it may be reproduced, stored in a retrieval system, or transmitted, in any form or by any means, electrical, mechanical, electrostatic, magnetic tape, photocopying, recording or otherwise, without the prior written permission of the author.

ISBN: 978-978-8431-61-9

DEDICATION

This book is dedicated to my parents:
Chief Josiah Akinola,
the late Oisa of Oke-Ikere from 1946-1979
and my mother,
Madam Janet Aderinko Akinola.

CONTENTS

Dedication v

Acknowledgements ix

Foreword xi

Preface xiii

Introduction xv

Chapter One

Colonialism and the Heritage of Multipartism, 1914-1951   1

Chapter Two

Pre-Independence Party Politics (1951-1960): The Emergence of "Tripartism"   25

Chapter Three

Post-Independence Party Politics (1960 1966): An Era of Crises and Shifting Alliances   45

Chapter Four

The Military Interlude and Events of Consequence to the Party System, 1966-1979   65

Chapter Five

Post-Military Party Politics, 1979 to 1983:
The Scramble for the Presidency   85

Chapter Six

From Manufacturing A Two-Party System to a
Potential Two-Party System   105

Bibliography   137

Index   145

ACKNOWLEDGEMENTS

I am grateful to Professor Charles W. Harris who not only encouraged me to research into the subject of party development in Nigeria, but also supervised the research. He is one great professor of Political Science whose love for others transcends class, ethnicity and race. I am also grateful to Professors Babalola Cole and Morris Levitt, both of Howard University, who were members of the research committee. I appreciate the affections of Professors Anthony Kirk-Greene of Oxford University and Ladipo Adamolekun, two world-class scholars, who, among others, enthusiastically encouraged this publication.

My gratitude also goes to Mathew Smith and Thomas Mayo of Electric Reads as well as Kolade Mosuro of Mosuro The Booksellers, Ibadan, for competent editorial inputs and suggestions. I appreciate the invaluable professional contributions of my publisher, Chief Joop Berkhout, to the publication of this book.

Finally, I say THANK YOU to my wife and children for their love, loyalty, and support.

FOREWORD

As part of his finely crafted and constructed writings, Anthony Akinola here brings another book to his already expanding library of major Akinola publications. In it, too, he introduces a password of mini-triumph among those taking part, namely the attractive unifying phrase "Nigeria is great". May I be modest enough to offer an alternative to Akinola's readers, not so much "Nigeria is great" but rather the alternative conclusion that "Nigerians are great". Such recognition, may I suggest to Akinola, is often recognition by Nigerians among Nigerians of how they might view the Nigerians' own viewpoint of what it is that gives today's Nigerians their treasured material confidence.

Having spent over fifty years in an essentially Nigerian social context (mainly the academic one) among Nigerian undergraduates and graduate students, co-teaching with Nigerian colleagues, co-resident in classrooms, libraries and laboratories, predominantly among fellow Nigerians although by no means necessarily working inside Nigeria, has enriched my family life. By the time I returned from having spent fifty years in a Nigerian context, I was left with no doubt in my mind that Nigerians were indeed supremely lucky, not because Nigeria is indeed great but because, even more convincingly, "Nigerians are great". Spend weeks and months among Nigerians, in every corner of their academic activities from first year undergraduate, third year finalist, prize-winner, professor, head of department or distinguished visiting lecturer, all the way with your colleagues alongside. In the event, the more we met and get to know and write about the people of Nigeria, the greater the influence (conscious or unconscious) of Nigerians when they meet to work and play together in Nigeria.

Be it history or trade which displays priority in the day's events, Nigerians often seem as creative as they are active and friendly. They are also a most resilient people.

Akinola's excellent political history book reveals the ups and downs of Nigeria since its creation by the British in 1914. A presidential election is due in 2015, with all its implications; I wish the friendly peoples of Nigeria well as their nation begins its journey into the second century of its existence.

Anthony Kirk-Greene
University of Oxford
March 2014.

PREFACE

A major development occurred in Nigerian democratic politics when political parties of the progressive ideological persuasion or assumption surrendered their individual liberties and coalesced in a broad-based political party, the All Progressives Congress, setting the stage for future electoral contests in which two strong political parties would be involved. The political party that has controlled the presidency since 1999, the Peoples Democratic Party, is perceived to be conservative-inclined.

The perception that one group is conservative and the other progressive, has its roots in colonial rule. The erstwhile politicians of southern Nigeria, where Christian missionaries had great influence, viewed themselves to be progressive, while their counterparts of the major political party from the Muslim-dominated north were the conservatives.

True to this ideological perception, southern politicians had tended to advocate accelerated development while those of the north had preferred the rather cautious approach. However, the progressives had been less united as splinter "progressive" parties existed among the different ethnic groups. In contrast, conservative-oriented political parties had been relatively more purposeful and had provided leadership throughout Nigeria's democratic life.

The recent merger of the progressives, a development compelled by the unifying influence of the presidency, presents the prospect of a more competitive electoral politics in the years ahead. I had envisaged this development, once Nigeria changed from the parliamentary system to the presidential one, prompting a thesis that Nigeria would achieve a two-party system. Specifically, it was argued in the thesis, "Party Coalitions and the Trend Towards a Two-Party System in Nigeria", that the institution of the presidency would compel people of different backgrounds to coalesce in broad-based political parties.

I had wanted to publish the thesis immediately after it was successfully defended at the Department of Political Science, Howard University, in 1983 but was discouraged from doing so because the democratic experiment was terminated by the military in December of that year. However, subsequent events have justified the need for an updated version. First, a military government sought to impose a two-party structure by fiat, not least because of the tendencies exhibited in a history of party coalitions. Secondly, the merger of the progressive parties confirmed my thesis as proved.

However, Party Coalitions in Nigeria – History, Trends, and Prospects – takes the reader through the political evolution of Nigeria. The narrative should be welcoming both to those interested in Nigerian history and politics and the inquisitive scholars in the field of comparative politics.

Anthony Akinola
Oxford, January 2014.

INTRODUCTION

Two factors are critical to understanding the nature of party coalitions in Nigeria. The first derives from the country's heterogeneity, while the second is the perception of ideological differences amongst its politicians. Each of these factors will be explained in sequence.

The factor of heterogeneity is owed, in part, to Nigeria's origins as a creation of British colonialists. Nigeria is multi-ethnic, with quite a few of its component units large enough to constitute viable nations on their own. Languages vary within these units and so too do cultural and religious practices. Political parties have tended to revolve around nationalities, making coalitions inevitable for political governance at the federal level.

There is also a thin line of ideological perceptions or assumptions by Nigeria's politicians. There is the perception that one group is 'progressive', the other 'conservative'. These perceptions have their origins in colonial rule; particularly thanks to the activities of Christian missionaries. The erstwhile politicians of southern Nigeria, where Christian missionaries had great influence, viewed themselves as progressive, while their counterparts from the Muslim-dominated North were the conservatives. However, these right and left-wing divides now cut across the various ideological divisions of the country and are quite often taken up or discarded in acts of political opportunism.

Be that as it may, the nature of party coalitions in Nigeria is explicable in the context of the political system the country has experimented with during its democratic history. Nigeria inherited the parliamentary system of government from the British colonial masters but now operates an American-type presidential/congressional system. The pattern of party coalitions differs considerably in the practices of the two political systems.

The parliamentary system of government, with its attributations of "Government" and "Opposition", invites the coalition of political parties following the conclusion of an election. The party or parties that would form the government must have the majority of seats in the legislature. In Nigerian society, where factional political parties characterised the early parliamentary era, post-electoral coalitions of contrasting or conflicting political parties have dominated.

However, Nigeria's experience with the presidential system of government contrasts with that of the parliamentary alternative. Unlike the post-electoral coalitions concomitant with the parliamentary experience, coalitions need to be consummated prior to a presidential election by those who seek to control the presidency. This new reality for Nigerian politics has altered the pattern of political party coalitions in the country. The more purposeful political parties now seek to broaden their bases of support; the result is that, today, Nigeria boasts two political parties – the People's Democratic Party (PDP) and the All Progressives Congress (APC) – that qualify as national political parties.

The Nigerian party system is still evolving; a comprehensive appraisal of the political history of this important African nation will help the reader in understanding the extent of current achievements and the travails of nation-building in a severely divided nation. Hence, this book is tailored to the reader with an eye on the history and politics of Nigeria.

Chapter One focuses on the establishment of the Nigerian state, with emphasis on the system of 'indirect rule' initially employed by the colonialists in the administration of their vast colony. The activities of Christian missionaries, restricted as they were to non-Muslim areas, have continued to have implications for unity and social integration in Nigerian society.

Chapter Two relates the initial struggles among the political parties in the period before independence (1951-1960). Discussed, among other topics, are the influences of the constitutional changes – the Macpherson Constitution of 1951 and the Lyttleton Constitution of 1954 – on the emergence of three dominant political parties representing each of the then-three regions (East, North, and West). The patterns of party coalitions before the attainment of independence are also discussed.

Chapter Three covers the post-independence era. The patterns and motives of party alliances are highlighted. The climax of this chapter is the illustration of the various crises that not only culminated in military intervention but also paved the way for the emergence of two trans-ethnic umbrella groups of political parties – the Nigerian National Alliance (NNA) and the United Progressive Grand Alliance (UPGA), thus providing an important framework for subsequent party development.

Chapter Four is an attempt to demonstrate that, although political party activities were proscribed during the military period of 1966-1978, certain contributions were made which are of significant effect to party development. Such contributions include the demarcation of Nigeria into smaller states and the adoption of a presidential constitution.

Chapter Five provides an analysis of the impact of the presidency on political party development. It discusses the move towards a two-party system and the attempts of the "progressive" parties to merge in order to be able to counter-balance the influence and power potential of a dominant political party seemingly of the conservative persuasion, the National Party of Nigeria (NPN).

Finally, Chapter Six concludes the book with current developments; the military government's imposition of a two-party structure by fiat, the emergence of two broad-based political parties, the PDP and the APC, and how these developments led towards a two-party system for Nigeria. Of course, there remains the discussion of whether this potentially historic achievement can be sustained.

CHAPTER ONE

COLONIALISM AND THE HERITAGE OF MULTIPARTISM, 1914-1951

> *Nigeria is a vast country in both size and population. It is an amalgam of diverse ethnic groups, large and small, with its own language, customs and culture. Therefore the Nigeria of today owes its origin only to the British Administration.*[1]

The above summary presents an ethnological picture of Nigeria. The history of Nigeria is a history of British commercial adventurism. The various kingdoms: Yoruba, Ibo, and Hausa, among others, were occupied at different times, but were ganged together in a progressive merger which culminated in the grand amalgamation of the Northern and Southern protectorates on 1 January, 1914.

---

1. Oluwole Idowu Odumosu, *The Nigerian Constitution: History and Development*, (London: Sweet and Maxwell, 1963), p. 205.

By 1900, when conquest had almost been accomplished, the country was administered 'either directly or indirectly' in three separate units:

(1) The colony and protectorate of Lagos, [which consisted of the areas of authority of the present six states in the South-Western geo-political zone, excluding former Egba Division].

(2) The protectorate of Southern Nigeria [which comprised roughly the areas of authority of the present five states in the South-Eastern and six states in the South-Southern geo-political zones, respectively].

(3) The protectorate of Northern Nigeria [which was more or less the same as the present nineteen states of North-Eastern, North-Western, and North Central geo-political zones, as well as the capital territory, Abuja. [2]

The colony and protectorate of Lagos and the protectorate of Southern Nigeria were merged into a simple unit known as the Protectorate of Southern Nigeria in 1906. This grand amalgamation, which led to the birth of Nigeria in 1914, was compelled by financial circumstances. The Northern protectorate could not generate sufficient funds to maintain its own administration "in spite of the annual grants from the Imperial Treasury and from the Southern Administration," while on the other hand, the South had a satisfactory fund due to its rapidly developing trade. The

---

2. Obafemi Awolowo, *The People's Republic* (Ibadan: Oxford University Press, 1968), pp. 15-16.* See Appendix III for current arrangement.

immediate objective of amalgamation was therefore to relieve the Imperial Treasury of its growing commitment to the North.[3] It can therefore be inferred that if the North had been economically viable enough to stand on its own, amalgamation would probably not have taken place.

Nigeria consists of innumerable ethnic groups; there are more than one hundred, of which Hausa-Fulani, Yoruba, and Ibo are the largest. Languages vary with these groups, and so do religious practices. The prominent religions are Muslim, Christian, and indigenous African beliefs. As one author sums up, "When it comes to diversity, Nigeria is probably second to none in the whole World."[4] Another author, after weighing all the various contradictions concocted into a single entity by the British administration, contends that:

> ...marked differences in language, religion, custom and culture could not be obliterated by the mere fact of amalgamation. It could therefore be said that the real importance of amalgamation was that it created the framework within which a single virile and united nation could emerge in the future.[5]

The Indirect Rule System

The inherent problem in amalgamation was immediately felt by the Governor-General, and the architect of Nigeria's amalgamation, Sir Frederick Lugard. The political

---

3. James O. Ojiako, *Nigeria, Yesterday, Today, And...* (Onitsha, Nigeria: Africana Educational Publishers (Nig.) Ltd., 1981), p. 9.
4. Chief Lai Joseph, *"Nigeria's Elections: The Bitter Truth,"* (Lagos: Nmogun Commercial Printers Limited, 1981), p. 9.
5. Odumosu, *The Nigerian Constitution*, p. 17.

governance of these diverse groups could only be facilitated through the application of the 'indirect rule system,' which sought to govern through the existing traditional administrations. C.S. Whitaker presents a clear illustration of the strategy of indirect rule in the following words:

> *Lugard perceived that a solution for his problems presented itself in the form of the already effectively functioning system of government, which by then offered such obvious additional advantages of religious justification for authority, a formal code of law (the Islamic sharia), specialised judicial constitutions, a more centrally controlled apparatus of administration, the custom of taxation, and above all, the people's habit of obeying state authority...*[6]

Lugard divided the territory into units called Provinces, each headed by a British Resident. These Provinces were further subdivided into Administrative Divisions, with a District Officer in charge of each. Organisation at the grassroots level was entrusted to the paramount chiefs or natural rulers, who were assisted by their subordinate chiefs.

Indirect rule was a huge success in the North, where the conditions experimented upon had existed for a very long time. In the Yoruba land, the experiment met initial confrontations in some areas, but such impediments were quickly suppressed by the British, and the natural rulers, who loved the new administrative power bestowed upon them by their colonial masters, quickly established their grip over the system. In most parts of Ibo land, there were

---

6. C.S. Whitaker, Jr., *The Politics of Tradition, Continuity and Change in Northern Nigeria, 1946-1966* (Princeton, New Jersey: Princeton University Press, 1970), p. 27.

no natural rulers, but Lugard, in his desperate bid to administer the area with minimum human and financial resources, resorted to 'manufacturing' some artificial 'natural rulers', known as 'warrant chiefs', from some influential members of the community. After an initial success, the practice was to receive a setback when the privilege became extended to some dubious and inconsequential characters. Although Lugard left Nigeria in 1918, his system of indirect rule, "with various degrees of malpractice and readjustment was on the forward march throughout the country, except Lagos."[7] The system lasted until the early 1950's.

The year 1939 is another significant date in Nigeria's history. The Southern provinces were bifurcated into the Western and Eastern provinces, each under a Chief Commissioner, with headquarters at Ibadan and Enugu. These two provinces, together with the Northern province 'headquartered' at Kaduna, marked the birth of three geographically distinct and politically hostile cultures.

Considering the objective of this tripartite arrangement, politically designed to keep Nigeria perpetually within the British sphere of influence, a writer asserts:

> *It must be noted that this political arrangement by the British was not necessary. They could, for instance, have carved out a region for the Kanuri in the north-east, since that area was never captured by the Fulani. They could also have carved out a region for the Yoruba of Ilorin and the Tiv of the Benue, since their areas were geographically and*

---

7. Awolowo, *The People's Republic,* p. 24.

> *ethnologically distinct from the Hausa area, further North.*[8]

It is not the purpose of this book to dwell on the success or failure of the 'indirect rule' system, or to provide its detailed operation. What is important here about the system is that it provided an infrastructure for the multiplicity of political parties in Nigeria. It is to the discredit of the colonial administrators that having brought a group of diverse cultures together in their attempt at 'amalgamation', their system of 'indirect rule' perpetuated the preservation of cultural differences. If the British had attempted a monolithic approach to the administration of the country, the pattern of political parties that emerged at the inception of nationalism would probably have been other. With the various cultures neither exposed to each other, nor given a direction of unity, suspicion was likely to develop. Irving Leonard Markovitz postulates a similar view in his analysis of the historical impact of colonialism and imperialism on Africa:

> *Colonial policies and structures of rule differed among the European powers and over time these policies conditioned the nature of the nationalist movements that emerged in Africa before independence [...] The objectives and methods of imperialism also affected the continuities between ongoing African indigenous systems and post independence.*[9]

---

8. Adewale Ademoyega, *Why We Struck* (Evans Brothers Nigeria Publishers-Limited, 1981), p. 3.
9. Irving Leonard Markovitz, *Power and Class in Africa: An Introduction to Change and Conflict in African Politics*, (New Jersey: Prentice-Hall, Inc., 1977), p. 59.

Colonialism thrives in division. A policy of national unity or national consciousness, if pursued by the British, might have resulted in a violent and untimely extermination of the benefits of colonialism. One can then understand, from the perspective of political realism, why the British administrators preferred to "refer to their subjects as Yorubas, Ibos, or Hausas, and not as Nigerians."[10] The psychological effect was that loyalty to the ethnic group took precedence over national loyalty.

Unequal Educational Development: Government and Missions

The dual approach to education must be considered as the greatest legacy of disunity bequeathed to Nigeria by the British administration. If, for a long time after independence, Nigerians found it difficult to relate to themselves without suspicion, this foundation of unequal educational development merits substantial blame. Education, being a supreme force of socialisation and integration, would appear to have been deliberately ignored as a tool for unifying the intermixture of cultures loosely compounded under amalgamation. The reason for this cannot be gainsaid: balkanisation ensures the continuity of imperialistic objectives.

Education in Southern Nigeria was spearheaded by the missionary organisations "which have established village teachers, primarily with a view to training natives in the principles of Christian religion."[11] Education in the

---

10. S.A. Akintoye, *Emergent African States: Topics in Twentieth Century African History* (London: Longman Group Ltd., 1976), pp. 3-4.

11. Raymond Leslie Buell, *The Native Problem in Africa* (New York: The MacMillan Company, 1928), Vol.1, p. 728.

North took a different dimension. The missionaries were discouraged from entering the North, except for non-Muslim areas, "lest they should offend Islamic susceptibilities."[12]

Education in the Muslim areas of the North was in government hands. The hostility of the Emirs to Western education was appreciated and respected by the British administrators, and therefore education was designed to accommodate their religion and language. The South, on the other hand, developed a highly receptive attitude to Western values and ideas, to the extent that any attempt to provide a system of education which differed from that given to Europeans was considered "an attempt to hold them in a kind of intellectual serfdom."[13] Letters of appointment to Emirs were not without a promise from Lord Lugard, that the government would "studiously refrain from any action which will interfere with the exercise of the Mohammedan religion by its adherents, or which will demand of them action that is opposed to its precepts."[14] After the departure of Lugard in 1918, his successors would later hold this pledge to mean a total exclusion of Christian missionaries from the North. In a letter written in 1919, the colonial office justified this "new interpretation" on two grounds:

> *First, because of the pledge to the Emirs, which should be constructed in the light of the fact that "Christian missionaries are of the same race and creed as higher officials of the protectorate*

---

12. Ken Post, *The New States of West Africa* (Middlesex, England: Penguin Books Ltd., 1964), p. 47.
13. Buell, *The Native Problem in Africa*, p. 732.
14. Ibid., p. 733.

government; and that if they should be granted land, etc.," the natives would arrive at the conclusion "that the missionary propaganda had the support of the Government and that the Government was false to its pledges;" second, because any action which weakened the authority of the Muslim religion would weaken the authority and prestige of the Emirs with the result that the present system of indirect rule would be imperilled.[15]

Because of the higher stake of preserving the indirect rule system, it was always unlikely that the British would persuade religious adherents to attend government schools. Government involvement in Northern schools was therefore to little effect. The total attendance of the fifty-two government schools was less than two thousand – a figure far below attendance in the South.[16]

The impact of this ambiguous educational approach on Nigeria's party system can be viewed from two perspectives: first, the entrance of Christian missions to the non-Muslim areas of the North effected an antagonistic culture to the conservative culture of the Muslim areas; second, because the South had produced more educated men, well-nurtured in the dynamics of Western democracy, a feeling of suspicion and political incompatibility was developed by the North against the South. These effects, coupled with other tribal contradictions, would later translate into different political loyalties.

---

15. Buell, *The Native Problem in Africa*, p. 734.
16. Annual Report of the Education Department, Northern Provinces, 1925, p. 14.

The Emergence of Political Parties

Although local political organisations started in Nigeria as far back as 1922,[17] this chapter, and indeed, book will be concerned with political parties in their struggles for independence and, consequently, their struggles among themselves, for political power. Such political parties emerged during and after the Second World War.

If World War II was a disaster for Europe, it proved to be a blessing for some of the colonies, including Nigeria. Europe became economically weakened, to the extent that the wisdom of managing overseas territories was questioned. Consequently, there was a need to hasten withdrawal from overseas commitments. At this point, the policy of self-government and ultimate independence for Nigeria became the declared objective of the British colonial masters. Nigerians who had received higher education in Britain and America became the major voice for independence. This group of educated men, having observed the politics of these nations (America and Britain) had come to appreciate the role of political parties in the governmental process. Apart from the common goal of independence, the desire for influence and prestige associated with office provided an additional impetus for competition between political parties and among individuals.

The diverse nature of Nigeria expressed itself in the nature of political parties that proliferated in the political arena in the search for political power. For the purpose of this chapter, discussions will be limited to those political

---

17. Nnamdi Azikiwe, *The Development of Political Parties in Nigeria* (London: Office of the Commissioner in the United Kingdom for the Eastern Region of Nigeria, 1957), p. 5.

parties which impacted on the politics of Nigeria. Such political parties were: the National Council of Nigeria and the Cameroons (NCNC), the Action Group (AG), the Northern People's Congress (NPC), and to some extent, the Northern Elements Progressive Union (NEPU) and the United Middle Belt Congress (UMBC). A brief analysis of the background and objectives of each of these parties is important for understanding their subsequent behaviour.

(a) The N.C.N.C

The National Council of Nigeria and the Cameroons, as the name implies, sought a national character. It was formally inaugurated on August 26, 1944, with the following objectives:

(1) To extend democratic principles and to advance the interests of Nigeria and the Cameroons under British mandate.

(2) To organize and collaborate with all its branches throughout the country.

(3) To adopt suitable means for the purpose of imparting political education to the people of Nigeria with a view to achieving self-government.

(4) To afford the members the advantages of a medium of expression in order to secure political freedom, economic security, social equality and religious toleration in Nigeria and the Cameroons under British mandate, as a member of the British Commonwealth of Nations.[18]

---

18 Azikiwe, *The Development of Political Parties in Nigeria*, p. 10.
*   *The West African Pilot* which was founded in 1937, became the chief organ for the propagation of NCNC ideas.

The National Council of Nigeria and the Cameroons, which later became known as the National Council of Nigerian Citizens, was led by Herbert Macaulay and Dr Nnamdi Azikiwe. The party received the support of Nigerian workers by its overt support for their cause during the strike of 1945. Until 1951, the NCNC was the only political party which claimed to be national. It was later identified with the Ibos of Eastern Nigeria.

Thomas' Regionalisation Theory

The 1946 Richards Constitution, the provisions of which will be briefly discussed later, did not succeed. The failure of the constitution was a pointer to the fact that "tribal diversities must be given sufficient consideration in any future constitution."[19] Apart from this, the constitution was considered ineffective as far as a change in the seat of political power was concerned.

By 1948, Chief Bode Thomas, a lawyer, had started to postulate a theory which sought to divide Nigeria into three regions. The significant impact of this theory on political party development makes it appropriate to present some of its main excerpts:

> *I believe that Nigeria must be better organised politically than it is today. The point is whether such organization should be based on a unilateral system or that three political bodies be set up on a regional basis to serve the needs of the East, West and North, respectively. They may be described as regional political parties and will deal exclusively with matters affecting their respective zones.*

---
19. Odumosu, *The Nigerian Constitution,* pp. 49-52.

> I believe that the latter suggestion, novel as it may sound, will serve the need of the country better. These three bodies may join up at the top and form a council for Nigeria which will be competent to tackle any matter that may affect the country generally. Some of the advantages of this system are:
>
> (1) It will give to the persons directly concerned an exclusive right to determine issues which are purely their own local affairs.
>
> (2) Leaders will be produced from each organization who will join together to accept whatever political responsibilities might be granted Nigeria in the near future.
>
> (3) The Northerners who have already been suspicious of the Southerners will at least be satisfied that there is no intention on the part of the Southern *Kafiris* to dominate the North or to interfere in their domestic affairs.[20]

This theory guided the philosophical development of, in particular, the Action Group (AG)

(b) The A.G.

The birth of the Action Group was formally announced on 21 March, 1951, in Nigerian newspapers, although Chief Obafemi Awolowo, leader of the party, revealed that the formation of the party had taken place one year before the

---

20. Azikiwe, The Development of Political Parties in Nigeria, pp. 15-17.

public announcement was made. The Action Group is a transformation of a cultural organisation, EGBE OMO ODUDUWA, which was founded in 1947. Awolowo's message to the founding fathers was illustrative of the nature and immediate objective of the party:

> ... to devise plans for organizing the people of the Western Region so that they may be able to play an influential and effective role in the affairs of Nigeria under the New Constitution.[21]

The Action Group started as a well-organised and disciplined political party. Contrasting the AG with the NCNC, Professor Odumosu comments:

> Unlike the NCNC, the AG started with individual membership, it confronted the people with a definite programme by way of policy papers on subjects such as education, health, agriculture and local government.[22]

This programmatic distinction of the Action Group, and the consistency with which such programmes were emphasised and pursued, is worth noting. Until 1955, the Bode Thomas regionalisation theory was noted to have philosophically guided the Action Group. However, following the dictates of public opinion and the need to extend beyond its Yoruba borders, the party was compelled to modify its regional rigidity.[23]

---

21. Obafemi Awolowo, *Awo: The Autobiography of Chief Obafemi Awolowo,* (Cambridge: University Press, 1960), p. 214.
*   The *Daily Service* eventually became the mouthpiece of the Action Group.
22. Odumosu, *The Nigerian Constitution,* p. 205.
23. Azikiwe, *The Development of Political Parties in Nigeria,* p. 18.

Party Development in Northern Nigeria

Nationalism was late to start in the North. Coleman gives three reasons that eventually helped bring it into existence. First, nationalism in the South was said to have some stimulating effect on potential nationalistic Northerners. Second, Northerners who were privileged to visit the United Kingdom during the period 1945-1950, returned as exponents of new ideas. Third, and perhaps the most preponderant of all, was the realisation that the North was educationally and materially inferior to the South and, therefore, the legitimate fear that the North might be subordinate to the South in an independent Nigeria.[24]

(c) The N.P.C.

The Northern People's Congress merits some detailed discussions for three reasons: First, the development of political parties in the North, with the attended suspicion of the Emirs and the British, exposes the difference in character between the North and the regions of the South, where such constraints were almost nil. Second, the motives and objectives of the party help to explain the contradictions harboured by an amalgamation of incompatible cultures. Third, the NPC is unique among the three major parties. The party was committed to Northern regionalism, not only by name identification, but also by its stated principles; yet it was the most powerful

---

24. James S. Coleman, *Nigeria: Background to Nationalism* (Berkeley and Los Angeles: University of California Press, 1963), p. 367.

* The *Gaskiya T'afikwabo* of the North, although a Government publication, was practically the mouthpiece of the NPC.

party, with various opportunities to exert meaningful influence in both domestic and external politics.

The Katsina College Old Boys' Association, launched in 1939, was the precursor of political parties in the North. The Association, with such aims as, "(1) to ooze out imperialism, (2) to break down the idea of sole Native Authority, and (3) to prevent domination by Southerners,"[25] did not thrive in a Northern Nigeria, where non-traditional principles were frowned upon by the powerful traditional rulers and by the colonial masters, who were themselves beneficiaries of highly-institutionalised traditions. Apart from the suspicions of the establishment, the members of the Association were also employees of the colonial government or native administrations, and as such, maintaining such radical principles was tantamount to the loss of employment benefits. Because of these impediments, this association died a natural death within two years of its inauguration.

And yet the 1940s proved the immortality of ideas. The former members of the Association became pioneers of various discussion groups aimed at educating the masses in several Northern towns. However, the extent to which the basic opportunities of democracy could be used is revealed below:

> *Groups that displayed prudence and moderation were tolerated by the Native Authorities and the British, who nevertheless watched their activities closely. Those which came under the influence of radicals did not survive: the Zaria Friendly Society and the Bauchi Discussion Circle, for example.*

---

25 Whitaker, *The Politics of Tradition*, p. 356.

> *The Zaria Friendly Society was forced to disband when its founder, Malam Sa'a du Zungur, a Koranic scholar and noted nationalist (one of the handful of Northerners to take the bold step of joining a Southern nationalist party - the NCNC - of which he was general secretary from 1948 to 1951) used its platform to attack the system of Native Administration. Similarly, official recognition was withdrawn from the controversial Bauchi Discussion Circle by the British Resident who had helped initiate it, when his salary and that of the Emir of Bauchi came up for discussion in the presence of both.[26]*

The year 1948 marked the eventual coagulation of the various organisations into a "region-wide cultural organisation called the Northern People's Congress (Jami'iyyar Mutanen Arewa), the NPC." The birth of the NPC was the merger of "two groups founded earlier the same year (Jami'iyyar Arewa at Zaria and the Jami'iyyar Mutanen Arema A'Yau at Kaduna)." Dr R.A.B. Dikko, a Christian and the North's first medical doctor, became its President.[27]

The following are the stated objectives of the NPC:

(1) Regional autonomy within one Nigeria;

(2) Local government reform within a progressive emirate system based on tradition and custom;

(3) The voice of the people to be heard in all the councils of the North;

(4) Drive for education throughout the whole North,

---

26. Ibid., p. 356.
27. Ibid., p. 357.

laying due emphasis on the improvement of the social, economic and cultural life of the people;

(5) Eliminate bribery and corruption in every sphere of Northern life;

(6) Eventual self-government for Nigeria with Dominion status within the British Commonwealth;

(7) Membership of the NPC is open to all people of Northern descent, whether as individuals or as a political party.

(8) Industrial and economic development of the Northern Region;

(9) One North, one people, irrespective of religion, rank or tribe.[28]

It was clear from these objectives that membership was not extended to the South, and that the preservation of Northern regionalism predominated national concerns. While the party promised "cautious friendship" to other ethnic groups,[29] its deference to traditional authority was emphatically stressed. There was a need to relieve the traditional leaders of the fear of an infiltration of *Kafiri* ideas' into the North and also to assure them that the new movement had no designs to usurp their 'God-given' authority:

---

28. Odumosu, *The Nigerian Constitution*, p. 210.
29. Ibid., p. 210

The Congress does not intend to usurp the authority of our natural rulers; on the contrary it is our ardent desire to enhance such authority wherever and whenever possible. We want to help our natural rulers in the proper discharge of their duties. We want to help them in enlightening the Talakawa (the peasant masses).[30]

(d) The N.E.P.U.

The NPC emerged as an admixture of conservatism and radicalism; the incompatibility of which was soon to surface. Those who could not tolerate the conservative philosophy of the NPC were soon to filter themselves out for a formation of a reform-oriented party known as the Northern Elements Progressive Union (NEPU).

The founders of this party were of relatively different social backgrounds. They were "of better than average education,"[31] and were mostly employed in non-governmental institutions, hence their relative indifference to the possibility of employment pressures and other forms of reprisals.

The NEPU, which was the first to declare itself a political party in the North, was inaugurated in Kano on August 8, 1950. The party became closely associated with the nationalist NCNC and was led by Malam Aminu Kano, who was known to be the protégé of Zungur.

This preamble presents the principles behind the formation of the party:

---

30. Ibid., p. 210.
31. Coleman, *Nigeria: Background to Nationalism,* pp. 358-359.

> *The Northern Elements Progressive Union is a Northern Party with democratic ideals and it is absolutely divorced from tribal and religious prejudices. It stands for the welfare of the people of Northern Nigeria and to establish sound social, economic and political justice to ensure domestic tranquility and to secure liberty of thought and expression, equality of status and opportunity for all the people of Northern Nigeria, and to promote among them all real fraternity, to the safeguarding of the individual and the unity of the people.*[32]

The above preamble reveals one major difference between this party and the NPC. The objective of promoting equality of status is obviously unwelcome in a conservative environment, where traditional rulers demand and are accorded due respect by their subordinates. It should be noted that the NPC avowed to uphold this dignity without reservations. It is therefore clear from this ideological distinction that the NEPU could not grow into a major party without first altering the power position of its domineering rulers.

(e) The U.M.B.C.

The United Middle Belt Congress did not emerge until 1953. Although it was a relatively minor party, its uniqueness grew out of the single issue of state creation for which it stood.

The UMBC was an aftermath of a merger of the Middle Belt People's Party (MBPP) formed by Moses Rwang "at the

---

32. Dr. Nnamdi Azikiwe, *Selected Speeches of Dr. Nnamdi Azikiwe*, (London: Cambridge University Press, 1961), p. 329.

behest of the national executive of the NCNC" and the Middle Zone League (MZL), which was organised by David Lot.[33] The UMBC was later identified with Mr J. S. Tarka, who piloted the party as a strong ally of the Action Group.

The Macpherson Constitution

Most of the political parties, as already revealed in the history of their emergence, were formed along regional lines and strengthened by the nature of Nigerian federalism. William H. Riker describes Nigeria as the "only one of the ex-British federalisms that does not display the unification of a number of separate colonies no one of which would have been viable alone."[34] Each of the three regions was larger than most African countries. This special qualification also explains the uniqueness of Nigeria's multipartism.

The Richards Constitution of 1946, as noted earlier, met with failure. Governor Richards had considered necessary, "a constitutional framework covering the whole of Nigeria and a Legislative Council in which all sections of the community will be represented." The Legislative Council, consisting of an unofficial African majority, "had representatives from all over the territory and legislated for the country as a whole."[35] Each of the three regions had a House of Assembly (the North, in addition, had a House of Chiefs), the members of which consisted of an African majority, and were elected by the native authorities. The

---

33. Eme O. Awa, *Federal Government in Nigeria* (Berkeley and Los Angeles: University of California Press, 1964), pp. 100-101.
34. William H. Riker, Federalism: *Origin, Operation, Significance* (Boston and Toronto: Little, Brown and Company, 1964), p. 31.
35. Henri Grimal, *Decolonization: The British, French, Dutch and Belgian Empires, 1919-1963,* trans. Stephen De Vos (Boulder, Colorado: Westview Press, 1978), p. 302.

members, in turn, elected every new member of the Legislative Council.[36] The new constitution did not alter the political equation in favour of the aspiring nationalists, and was therefore attacked on the grounds that it:

> ...had been granted without seriously consulting opinion, since the Legislative Council had not been allowed to discuss it; it did not take account of the aspirations of the new elites and confirmed the supremacy of the chiefs at all levels; africanisation was not extended to the big administrative departments and denied the Africans any direct participation in public affairs.[37]

It was during this period of political dissatisfaction, in 1948, that Sir John MacPherson arrived, with a commitment to solving the political problems that had been created by the constitution. The result of his efforts was the MacPherson Constitution of 1951.

The MacPherson Constitution was a defeat to nationalist aspiration. The new constitution gave too much power to the regions, such that the main political leaders preferred to remain in their respective regions, while their 'able lieutenants' were sent to the less attractive centre. The highlight of the constitution was that the three regions would be maintained as political units, with their assemblies charged with the responsibility of electing members to the central legislature. The Legislative Council was replaced by a chamber of representatives with an African majority. The North controlled half of the seats.[38]

---

36. Ibid., pp. 301-302.
37. Ibid., p. 302.

The constitution received the approval of the highly regionalised NPC and AG, while the national-oriented NCNC frowned upon it.

The NCNC later degenerated into a regional party, and this constitution cannot be exonerated from responsibility for such an unfortunate move. In a circumstance where the centre was conspicuously unattractive, the tendency was for leaders to jealously guard their individual regions against any incursion by 'external' political parties. At this time, symbols of tribal antagonism were the mobilising tools employed to confine the influence of 'intruding' political parties to their regions of origin.

---

38   Ibid., p. 302-303.

CHAPTER TWO

PRE-INDEPENDENCE PARTY POLITICS (1951-1960): THE EMERGENCE OF "TRIPARTISM"

Prior to the MacPherson Constitution of 1951, most of the political parties had been formed, but the extent to which each could exert influence within the different geographical constituencies had not been tested. The regionalisation 'message' of the Constitution was, however, not ambiguous. Each of the major parties, with the exception of the National Council of Nigeria and the Cameroons (NCNC), concentrated its efforts on controlling the regional legislatures: the Action Group (AG), the Western; the Northern People's Congress (NPC), the Northern; and the NCNC, albeit begrudgingly, the Eastern.[39] Elections were held in December 1951, with the NPC and the NCNC winning decisively in the North and in the East respectively;

---

39. Okoi Arikpo, *Development of Modern Nigeria* (Baltimore: Penguin Books, 1967), p. 75.

while the position in the West was not immediately clear, although the AG "had claimed winning 44 of the 75 members elected indirectly from all constituencies except Lagos."[40] The five seats contested in Lagos, which was then a part of the Western legislature, had all been won by the NCNC, a close competitor with the A.G. for control of the West.[41]

The position in the West became clarified on January 7, 1952, when the Western House of Assembly convened for the first time. The NCNC team was headed by its national leader, Dr Nnamdi Azikiwe, who had contested the election from Lagos, while the A.G. team was led by Chief Obafemi Awolowo. It was apparently a major surprise to the NCNC leaders that some of the members elected on the party's platform had decided to cross over to the A.G. side, thus increasing the latter's strength to 49, for a convenient control of the Western House of Assembly. This episode would later be known in Nigerian politics as 'carpet-crossing.' According to an eye-witness account, this betrayal was so bitter that Chief Festus Okotie-Eboh and Chief T.O.S. Benson shed tears while Nnamdi Azikiwe, displaying the magnanimity of a great man, kept on smiling. Dr Azikiwe was later advised to "resign from the Western House of Assembly where he was regarded as a stranger and seek a

---

40. Ibid., p. 75.
    Lagos would later be separated from the Western legislature following the Lyttleton Constitution of 1954.
41. Richard L. Sklar, *Nigerian Political Parties: Power In An African Nation* (Princeton, New Jersey: Princeton University Press, 1963), p. 115.

seat in the Eastern House of Assembly" where he belonged.[42]

As a result of the 1951 elections, the NPC, the NCNC, and the AG were afforded the opportunity not only to provide regional ministers for the Executive Council, but also to nominate the four central ministers from the North, East, and West respectively. This initial victory marked the beginning of a three-party system in Nigeria, as each of the parties began to consolidate an effective control over its areas of jurisdiction.

Towards an Eclipse of the MacPherson Constitution

The House of Representatives was composed of 68 members from the North, 34 each from the East and the West, 6 ex-officio members, and 6 nominated to represent special interests. Members from the regions were chosen by and from the respective Regional Assemblies.

The nationalist NCNC did not like the MacPherson Constitution right from its inception; and, spurred on by the episode in the Western House of Assembly, the militant members of the party were determined to bring it to an end.

Dr Azikiwe's determination to bring about the downfall of the Constitution did not receive the support of a majority of the NCNC ministers, most of whom were of the opinion that the Constitution should be given a fair trial.

---

42. Chief Dennnis Osadebay (GCON), "Party Alliance: It Happened Before," *Sunday Times,* March 21, 1982, p. 13.

   There were heated debates and antagonism between the *West African Pilot* of the N.C.N.C and the *Daily Service* of the Action Group. Although the two papers are now "defunct", a future study of their antagonism will throw a lot of light on party development in Nigeria.

Conferences were summoned to discuss various approaches, but such conferences were not adequately attended by party members. At this point, it was clear that a line had been drawn between the NCNC ministers of the Eastern and Central governments on the one hand, and non-ministerial, national leaders of the party on the other. A special convention of the party, summoned by the Central Working Committee, met at Jos in December 1952, but despite the fact that the NCNC claimed the allegiance of 74 out of the 80 members of the Eastern House, only two members were reported to have attended the special convention. Infuriated by this disloyalty, Dr Azikiwe declared at the convention that henceforth, ministers would "toe the party line or be disciplined."[43] It was decided at the convention that the constitution was unworkable, and that the ministers should resign.

Ministers in the East had lost the confidence of the House of Assembly; therefore, letters of resignation were tendered to the Lieutenant-Governor. However, before these letters could be acted upon, each of the ministers had written to countermand them, claiming that the letters were signed under duress. Using his discretion, the Lieutenant-Governor withheld the letters and the ministers were allowed to continue with their official duties. The Lieutenant-Governor's action was challenged in the law court by disenchanted members who felt that the ministers should have been relieved of their duties, but their applications "were all struck out by the court for want of prosecution."[44] In February 1953, most of these ministers

---

43. Sklar, *Nigerian Political Parties*, pp. 119-121.
44. Arikpo, *Development of Modern Nigeria*, pp. 76-77.

formed a new party, the National Independence Party (NIP), under the leadership of Professor Eyo Ita. The N.I.P.'s attempt to carry on as a minority government in the East led to a constitutional deadlock.[45]

Having failed to remove the ministers by constitutional means, the leaders of the NCNC resorted to different tactics. The provisions of the Standing Orders were exploited to paralyse the business of the House, resulting in an impasse on the passage of the annual Appropriation Bill. Outside the House, party supporters, with the encouragement of party leaders, harassed the ministers and created such a disturbing atmosphere that a dissolution of the House appeared to be the only appropriate solution to the crisis.[46] Employing the special provision of the constitution, the Eastern House was dissolved by the Lieutenant-Governor, and a fresh election arranged.

Disenchantment with the MacPherson Constitution was gaining equal momentum in the West. Power was gradually being absorbed by Nigerians, to the discontentment of British officials. The new constitution had begun to work some unanticipated wonders: the emergence of politics on party lines had not been envisaged.[47] The reactions of British officials seemed to be designed to thwart such progress, and undermine the authority of the new elites. An example of such behaviour was the decision to promote certain officials despite their efforts to oppose the key policies of the ruling Action Group. One of these policies

---

45. The Royal Institute of International Affairs, *Nigeria: The Political and Economic Background* (Oxford University Press, 1960), p. 47.
46. Arikpo, *Development of Modern Nigeria*, p. 77.
47. Obafemi Awolowo, *Awo: The Autobiography of Chief Obafemi Awolowo*, p. 227.

was the abolition of the title of 'District Officer' – a title that embodied the mystique of colonial administration – in favour of the new and symbolically undistinguished title of 'Local Government Inspector'.[48] The resultant disenchantment of the AG, complementing the frustration of the NCNC over the MacPherson Constitution, was strong enough to cultivate an alliance for the constitution's abrogation and, consequently, for a greater goal of self-rule.

While the intra-party crisis was going on in the East, the AG was provided with the opportunity to stake its claim for national leadership. Chief Anthony Enahoro of the Action Group, and a member of the House of Representatives, put forward a motion demanding the acceptance of the principle of "self-government by 1956."[49] This action was unsurprisingly supported by the NCNC members. An almost unique feature of politics in colonial territories is the unity which is often compelled by an ambition to oust a common enemy, the colonial masters. Such commonality of interest becomes so strong that ideology is muted. This was specifically the basis for the NCNC/AG co-operation after the political 'debacle' of January 7, 1952. Moreover, members of both parties had been exposed to the same political tutelage in the South, so that the somehow conservative and ill-prepared NPC from the North now appeared to be an incompatible partner for them.

The motion for self-government was seen by the NPC members as calculated against the North. The Southerners

---

48. Sklar, *Nigerian Political Parties*, p. 124.
49. Ibid., p. 126

were better educated, and in fact most of the commercial and top administrative jobs in the North were in Southern hands. It was realistically perceived by the Northern members that they were not yet prepared for any competition with the South. Although the NPC was not without an objective for self-rule, at this point in time, an extended period of apprenticeship under the colonial masters would appear to be their unanimous preference. Therefore, it was not unexpected when the NPC objected to the specification of a timetable "on the ground that it was first of all necessary for them to obtain the assent of the traditional authorities and other representatives of the Northern People."[50] The motion for self-rule was said to have been first discussed in the Council of Ministers, where it was agreed upon by a majority vote that ministers should abstain from debating or voting on the motion – a resolution that forced into resignation the Action Group ministers who had dissented. The NPC tabled a counter-motion which was deficient in specificity - it merely substituted 'as soon as practicable' for '1956.'[51] This counter-motion generated bitter exchanges from both inside and outside the House, to the extent that the NPC threatened to secede from the nation. Perhaps the threat could have actually been effected, if the North had been endowed with the economic wherewithal, and access to the sea. The resentment of Northerners at the provocation over the question of self-rule was, however, brutally expressed. A visit to Kano, two months later, by Action Group delegates, was interrupted with serious rioting,

---

50. Ibid., p. 126.
51. Coleman, *Nigeria: Background to Nationalism*, p. 399.

"which resulted in 277 casualties, including 36 deaths (15 Northerners and 21 Southerners)".[52]

It was clear from the riotous debate in the House of Representatives that the welding force of national unity was apparently absent, and that "ministers tended to regard themselves as regional delegates with little feeling of collective responsibility."[53] This later development, coupled with the existing disgruntlement by other opinion centres, would seem convincing enough for the Colonial Secretary, Mr Oliver Lyttleton (later Lord Chandos). He suggested, in the House of Commons, on 21 May, 1953, that the constitution would "have to be withdrawn to provide for greater regional autonomy and the removal of powers of intervention by the Centre in matters which can, without detriment to other Regions, be placed entirely within regional competence."[54]

Towards A Federal Constitution

As a sequel to Lyttleton's proposal, a series of conferences was held in London in 1953 to discuss a new Constitution. The national-oriented NCNC was the last to be persuaded of the demand for greater regional autonomy. Divisions of power were concluded between the regions and the centre at the expense of the latter. In October 1954, a conference held in Lagos culminated in a Federal Constitution, sometimes referred to as the Lyttleton Constitution. The following are the highlights:

---

52. Ibid., pp. 399-400.
53. The Royal Institute of International Affairs, *Nigeria: The Political and Economic background,* pp.47-49.
54. Ibid., p. 49.

(1) It emphasized the federal aspect by sharing the legislative power between the regions and the centre. Finance, the administrative departments, the law courts and the municipal departments were regionalized;

(2) The governor-general was to retain the chairmanship of the central council of ministers, who would be selected by him from a list drawn up by the majority party and at a rate of three per region;

(3) It gave each region the possibility of obtaining full internal autonomy at a date of its own choice and, thereby, of developing each at its own pace. The East and West chose 1956; the North preferred to wait;

(4) It severed South Cameroon from the Eastern region and gave it a separate regional status.[55]

When it came to issues which might be more detrimental to one particular party or region in particular, other political parties or regions were quick to ally with one another. The question over the status of Lagos was to consummate an alliance between the NCNC and the NPC, both of which had supported the separation of Lagos from the West. Oliver Lyttleton, who was empowered at the London Conference to have a final say in the matter, decided in support of the NCNC and the NPC. The AG was disappointed at this decision, and therefore threatened to secede. Mr Lyttleton was furious, and queried, "Secede

---

55. Grimal, *Decolonization*, p. 304.

from what? Secede from what? Those who talk of secession must not forget that Her Majesty has interest in the matter."[56] The AG walked out of the Hall, and that was the end of the friendship which had been forged by the NCNC and the AG over the question of self-rule.

Federal Elections, 1954

It is worth mentioning here that the NCNC had been returned to the Eastern House with Dr Nnamdi Azikiwe as the Premier. Following the 1953 crisis in the East, the House of Assembly was dissolved, and a new election conducted, which swept the NCNC back into power with 72 out of the 97 seats. The NCNC was thus well-prepared to contest the Federal elections of 1954.

The Federal elections were conducted between October and December 1954 under different electoral systems. The direct ballot system was used in the East, West, and Lagos, while the electoral college system was used in the North, and in the Southern Cameroons.

One hundred and eighty-four seats were contested; the table below shows the number of seats won per party per region.[57]

---

56. Chief Dennis Osadebay, *Sunday Times,* March 21, 1982.
57. Ojiako, *Nigeria: Yesterday, Today and...,* p. 21.

	Northern Region	Western Region	Eastern Region	South Cameroons	Lagos	Total
N.P.C.	79	-	-	-	-	79
N.C.N.C.	-	23	32	-	1	56
A.G. UNIP Alliance	1	18	7	-	1	27
Kamerun National Congress	–	–	–	6	–	6
Others	12	1	3	–	–	16
	92	42	42	6	2	184

It was perhaps unanticipated by the Federal Constitution that a party would be strong enough to win the majority of Federal seats in more than one region, since each of the parties had come to be identified with the three regions. As the table above illustrates, the NCNC won the majority of seats in the East and in the West, while the NPC had also won 79 of the 92 seats in the North. It was only the AG that had not established an effective control over 'their' region, the West. An authoritative source tried to explain the failure of the AG:

> ...the Action Group's relative unpopularity was probably due to the increased taxation levied to pay for an ambitious programme of social improvement, and this, together with the NCNC's play upon tribal divisions in the non-Yoruba areas of the West,

> *combined to give the latter its unexpected victory in the region.*[58]

The Constitution required three ministers to be nominated from each region. Since no party had won the absolute majority of seats in the House of Representatives that would enable such party to nominate nine ministers in the Federal Government, it became the prerogative of the Governor-General to consult with the leaders of political parties which had won the majority of seats in each region, to appoint three ministers from each of the three main regions. The NPC nominated its three ministers from the North, while the NCNC was in a position to nominate the six ministers for the East and West.

The First Post-Electoral Coalition

The alliance forged over the question of Lagos was expressed in a post-electoral coalition between the NPC and the NCNC to form the Federal Government, while the AG became the official opposition.

The coalition was directly and indirectly a concoction of ideological incompatibles. The NCNC and the NPC, as the history of nationalism revealed, had nothing in common, while the NEPU (Northern Elements Progressive Union), which was an ally of the NCNC and a part of the coalition, was the radical party in the North, opposed to the NPC's conservatism. One might therefore be tempted to see the coalition as a temporary arrangement. Surprisingly, the coalition did not collapse, and, in fact, continued into the future.

---

58. The Royal Institute of International Affairs, *Nigeria: The Political and Economic Background,* p. 52.

Intra-Party Conflict in the East: The Action Group makes an Inroad

An intra-party dispute arose within the NCNC early in 1954. The details are not important to the focus of this book, but it is nevertheless necessary to give the highlights of this dispute because of its rather rewarding consequences for the AG.

The NCNC Government Chief Whip, Mr E.O. Eyo, accused the Premier of the East, and national leader of his party, Dr Nnamdi Azikiwe, of gross abuse of public office, and a motion was made in the Eastern House to that effect. Mr Eyo alleged that Azikiwe had allowed two million pounds of public money to be lodged in the African Continental Bank, where he had vested interest. A debate refused this motion in the House, on the grounds that there was 'a pending libel suit by the Premier against Mr Eyo.'[59]

A request for an independent tribunal to investigate the matter was made by the Governor, Sir Clem Pleass, but this request was refused by the Premier. The Colonial Secretary, Mr Lennox-Boyd, however, decided to investigate the matter by appointing a Commission of Inquiry under the Chief Justice of the Federation, Sir Stafford Foster-Sutton.

The fact that the matter was treated as political by the ruling NCNC was exploited by Dr Azikiwe. He exonerated himself by claiming that the British Banking Monopoly "had been unscrupulous in getting government business which should rightly have gone to African banks and that the inquiry had been instigated by British banking interests for fear of competition from the well-run African

---

59. Sklar, *Nigerian Political Parties,* p. 172.

Continental Bank."⁶⁰ This nationalist claim, as it would appear to be, was sufficient to keep Azikiwe's supporters loyal, in spite of the Foster-Sutton tribunal's conclusion that his conduct "had fallen short of the expectations of honest, reasonable people."⁶¹

The Eastern House was dissolved on January 19, 1957 at the request of the Regional Government, to enable an election to be held on the 15th of March. The NCNC retained control of the Government with 64 seats out of 84, while the AG, which previously had only one seat, increased its number to 13 to become the official opposition in the East. This gain was an added victory for the AG, which had, in the previous May, retained its control of the Western House with 48 out of 80 seats. The same election had seen the NCNC representation in the West increased from 13 to 32.

Federal Elections, 1959

The constitutional reforms were continued through a series of conferences. The East and the West decided to become self-governing in 1957, while the North preferred to wait until 1959. Both the NCNC and the NPC moved for independence in 1960, and the A.G. concurred - a harmony which culminated in the formation of a National Government composed of all three parties under the first Nigerian Prime Minister, Sir Abubakar Tafawa Balewa.⁶² The necessity to present a united front for independence seems to have motivated this coalition.

---

60. The Royal Institute of International Affairs, Nigeria: *The Political and Economic Background,* p. 54.
61. Ibid., p. 5.
62. John P. Mackintosh, *Nigerian Government and Politics* (Evanston: Northwestern University Press, 1966), p. 29.

With the approach of independence, the fear that the interests of minority groups would not be protected continued to grow. There was, therefore, an intensification of the demand by these minority groups that states be created before the exit of the British. Both the NCNC and the AG supported this issue, and it was indeed an electoral strategy for the latter in the 1959 campaigns. The NPC did not favour any attempt to create a new state out of the North, arguing that the North would be seriously harmed if the minorities, who constituted the bulk of administrative expertise in the Civil Service, were allowed to go. This argument seemed logical to the Willink Commission. The North had always received sympathetic consideration by the British, to the extent that when the Commission's report was reviewed by the Constitutional Conference in 1958, the Colonial Secretary ruled that, "if Nigeria would be independent in 1960, no new states could be created."[63]

The British could not be asked to postpone independence, but the Action Group decided to fight the 1959 election "on a platform calling for creation of more states before independence in 1960."[64] The AG would appear to have carefully selected this issue as a strategy of winning the votes of minority areas, since such agitation was country-wide. The mere fact that the A.G. was prepared to create a Midwestern Region out of the West gave credibility to this promise.

The NPC did not need to come to the South, and in fact it did not extend its membership to Southerners. The party was at a convenient position to contest 174 of the

---

63. Frederick A. O. Schwarz, Jr., Nigeria: The Tribes, The Nation, or The Race- The Politics of Independence (Massachusetts: The M.I.T. Press, 1965), p. 98.
64. Ibid., p. 99.

312 seats allocated to the North. If it could win all the seats in the North, it had surely secured the majority of Federal seats to enable it to control the National Government. The East and the West were allocated 73 and 62 seats, respectively. Both the NCNC and the AG were, therefore, in a dilemma, since they had to compete effectively for the seats in the North in order to be viable contestants for the position of Prime Minister.

There was much at stake in this election. Since it was an election preceding independence, it was considered a remarkable and monumental achievement for whichever party was able to form the government at that time. The added prestige of becoming the first Prime Minister of an independent Nigeria brought Dr Nnamdi Azikiwe and Chief Obafemi Awolowo, both Premiers of their respective regions, into the race for the Federal House.

The campaigns for the 1959 election were unprecedented in the annals of Nigerian politics. Southern efforts were directed to the seemingly impenetrable North. In all the regions, tribal awakening was the reliable tool for political mobilisation.

The coalition reached by the NCNC and the NPC after the Federal election of 1954 seemed to have made the two political parties more soft on each other, while the AG was now their common enemy. The Action Group mounted an expensive campaign, making use of helicopters, but such an extravagant show would later be used against it as the NPC vigorously and consistently asserted that, "the helicopters, and indeed all the Action Group's aggressive campaigning, were offensive to the Northern people."[65] The

---

65. Ibid., p. 103.

leader of the NPC, Sir Ahmadu Bello, who was made to take campaign actions he probably would never have resorted to, became more hostile, impressing upon the Northerners that Awolowo was contemptuous of Islam, and would ban it if he should come to power. Such an allegation could not be made against the NCNC, since it had a strong ally in an essentially Muslim party, the NEPU[66]

The powerlessness of the AG to create states in the context of Nigerian politics was categorically exposed by Chief Dennis Osadebay, an NCNC leader, thus reducing the issue into mere political rhetoric:

> *Owing to the constitutional position no one party in this country can create new Regions without the concurrence of at least one other major party. Owing to its habit of antagonising all and sundry, the Action Group will not be able to count on the NPC or NCNC to aid it. So those who want the Midwest Region created must support the NCNC and its good friend NPC who are the only parties capable of creating the Midwest region.*[67]

Considering the relative success made by the AG in the North – a success made possible by the minority areas – one would understand how potent the issue was at that time. The December 1959 election was conducted using the secret ballot in all the regions. In spite of the fact that no less than twenty-six parties were registered, the race,

---

66. Ibid., p. 109.
67. Ibid., p. 109.

as usual, was almost an exclusive preserve of the three major parties, as the table below indicates:[68]

Party	North	East	West	Lagos	Total
N.P.C	142	-	-	-	142
N.C.N.C./ N.E.P.U	8 (N.E.P.U)	58	21	2	89
A.G.	24	14	34	1	73
Independents	-	-	8	-	8
	174	72	63	3	312

The Second Post-Electoral Coalition

Since no single party had a majority of the seats, a coalitional government became inevitable. It was apparent from all indications that the NPC/NCNC coalition of 1954 would continue. Any possible coalition between the NCNC and AG, in spite of their seemingly more compatible policies, appeared to be undesirable. Such an alliance would have given credence to the Northern fear that the more progressive South would preclude the relatively backward North from the advantages of independence. It was therefore in the interest of national unity, and political harmony, that a government was not formed to the exclusion of the NPC

Moreover, events had presented the AG as the common enemy of both the NPC and the NCNC. The motion for self-rule in 1956 precipitated an antagonism between the AG

---

68. The Royal Institute of International Affairs, Nigeria: The Political and Economic Background, p. 63.

and the NPC. The aggressive 'intrusion' of the former into the latter's exclusive territory in the 1959 election only helped to increase existing enmity. The NCNC and the AG, on the other hand, were antagonistic competitors in the South, especially in the South-West. The NCNC had felt betrayed by the 'carpet crossing' of some of its members into the AG camp in January 1952. Despite the fact that there was nothing in common between the NPC and the NCNC, "the common desire to exclude the Action Group from Federal power"[69] was a sufficient cause for the continuity of the post-electoral coalition started in 1954.

Alhaji Abubakar Tafawa Balewa was invited by the Governor-General, Sir James Robertson, to form the Federal Cabinet. It was, however, made clear by the NPC that the most important position, that of Prime Minister, would not be compromised. Discussions were concluded with NCNC leadership prior to the formation of a new government; seven ministerial appointments were conceded to the latter, while the NPC retained ten.[70] The circle was completed when on November 16, 1960, Dr Nnamdi Azikiwe became the Governor-General of Nigeria. This compensation for joining the coalition was probably delayed due to the technical reason that Nigeria was still under the British administration:

> *It is announced that the Prime Minister of the Federation of Nigeria intend[s] to recommend to Her Majesty, The Queen, that Dr Nnamdi Azikiwe should be appointed as Governor-General of the Federation*

---

69. K.W.J. Post, *The Nigerian Federal Election of 1959: Politics and Administration in a Developing Political System* (Oxford: Oxford University Press, 1963), p. 441.
70. Ojiako, *Nigeria: Yesterday, Today and...*, p. 77.

after the retirement of Sir James Robertson on November 15, 1960. It has been ascertained that, if such a recommendation were made after Nigeria has achieved independence, Her Majesty would be pleased to accept it.[71]

The Action Group, under the leadership of Chief Obafemi Awolowo, became, for the second time, the formidable opposition at the Federal House.

---

71. Ibid., p. 92.

CHAPTER THREE

POST-INDEPENDENCE PARTY POLITICS (1960 1966): AN ERA OF CRISES AND SHIFTING ALLIANCES

Nigeria became independent on October 1, 1960. This monumental achievement ended a long period of colonial rule, which started with the cession of Lagos to Britain by King Docemo in 1861.

Independence meant that the erstwhile guidance by British administrators would no longer be required; successful management of peace and conflict now depended on the capability of the new political elites to justify preparedness for self-rule. Given the nature of Nigeria's heterogeneity, and the sombre truth that British administration had not made conscientious efforts to unify the various tribes, post-independence was bound to be testy and conflictual.

Meanwhile, a coalitional government had been formed by the NPC and the NCNC/NEPU, with the AG in the opposition. Aside from the fact that ideological differences between the parties in coalition were wide enough for many to doubt its continued success, the relationship between opposition and government was not the type that would limit politics in the house to 'war without violence'.

The Action Group maintained an uncompromising opposition, both in domestic and foreign policy matters, and was soon to endear itself to militant segments of the population. Among many of its criticisms was the critical apprehension of the Federal Government for "being too soft on colonialism, and for being closely aligned with the Western World".[72] The question of the Anglo-Nigeria Defense Pact was to receive vehement opposition from the Action Group, which considered the pact as a prerequisite for Nigeria's independence.[73] The Action Group described the Federal Government as a puppet of Britain and her NATO allies.[74] The consequent withdrawal of the pact was compelled when opposition to it extended to informed circles, especially students, who marched in Lagos for a demonstration of their disapproval.

Charges of neo-colonialism and corruption against the Government were not confined to Nigerian territories. Chief Awolowo, leader of the opposition, carried his criticisms wherever he went. In an address to Nigerian students in London, he repeated the same charges, without mincing his words. Considering Awolowo's criticisms as unbecoming and, moreover, that the charges were, ridiculously, made in an 'imperialist' territory, the Federal House of

---

72. Obafemi Awolowo, "Twelve months of Independence," *The Service*, II (Nov. 4, 1961), p. 29.
73. Parliamentary Debates, H. of R., Nov. 19, 1960, Col. 97.
74. Obafemi Awolowo, Twelve Months of Independence", *The Service*, II (Nov. 4, 1961), p. 29.

Representatives voted to censure him. Perplexed by Awolowo's behaviour, the Defence Minister, Alhaji Muhammadu Ribadu, asked if anyone could imagine Mr Gaitskell, Chief Awolowo's British counterpart, coming to Nigeria to criticise the policy of the British Government.[75]

Given the tribalised character of Nigerian political parties, it was commonplace to equate opposition from members of parliament to criticism coming from the West. When retaliation was therefore considered, methods ranged from "attacks on institutions based in the West,"[76] to such other measures that were capable of reducing the size, and consequently the political strength, of the region. For instance, there were contemplations in 1961 of extending the federal territory to the South and of the removal of part of Oyo Province to the North, but neither of these proposals could be effected, since "there was no popular demand for such changes."[77] The rationale for these considerations was that if the size and strength of the West were reduced, Action Group candidates in the detached constituencies would no longer have "all the machinery and patronage" of the West.[78] The creation of the Mid-West, however, presented an opportunity to punish the West.[79] There was already popular agitation for the transformation of that area into a separate region, and since such a creation was considered an advantage for the NCNC, the party became

---

75. Parliamentary Debates, H. of R , Nov. 29, 1961, Col. 3589; Nov. 30, 1961, Col. 3629.
76. John P. Mackintosh, "Federalim In Nigeria", *Political Studies,* Vol X, No.3 (1962), p. 236.
77. Ibid., p. 236.
78. John P. Mackintosh, "Federalism In Nigeria", *Political Studies,* X, p. 236.
79. Ibid., p. 236.

its sole advocate. It was not difficult for the co-operation of the NPC to be secured, since it was an opportunity to curtail the intransigence of a common enemy.

Creation of Mid-Western Region

The creation of the Mid-Western region should be regarded as the greatest conspiracy in Nigeria's 'trilateral' relations. It was not considered pressing or necessary to subdivide the North, despite the fact that its geographical area covered almost seventy-five percent of Nigeria's total land area, and its population more than that of the East and the West put together. There was also an old time agitation for the creation of Calabar-Ogoja-River States (COR) out of the Eastern region, an agitation which now seemed to have been ignored. Instead, it was the reduction of the West, which was then the smallest of the three regions, which became a priority of the ruling parties. The NCNC, which had made the question of new states an issue in its manifesto,[80] appeared no longer to see beyond the Mid-West. It was to the political disadvantage of the NCNC that the AG was gradually making an inroad into the Mid-West. In the 1959 Federal election, the party was able to win only 20 percent of the seats from the Mid-West, while conceding the rest to the NCNC By August 1960, when election to the Western House of assembly was conducted, the Action Group had succeeded in winning half of the Mid-West seats.[81] This intrusion into the stronghold of the embarrassed NCNC was, therefore, a reason for the NCNC to conclude that the trend towards A.G. domination of the

---

80. *Daily Times*, 2 August 1960, p. 13.
81. Schwarz, Jr., *Nigeria: The Tribes, The Nation, or The Race*, p. 125.

Mid-West was possible, due to the instruments of governmental power at the disposal of the latter in the West. The only constructive way to wrestle the Mid-West from Action Group takeover was to prune the area from the West.

The constitutional requirements for the creation of new states gave the NPC/NCNC coalition an opportunity to act from a position of strength. The NPC could singlehandedly obstruct the creation of any state in the federation. Five stages were required to be passed before any state/region could be created:

(1) Two-thirds of the members of both Houses of the Federal Parliament had to approve a resolution supporting the new region;

(2) Both the Houses of the regional legislature in a majority of the existing regions had to approve the same resolution;

(3) The Federal Parliament had to pass a more detailed bill providing for the creation of the new region;

(4) The bill had to be approved by resolutions of each legislative House in at least two regions; and

(5) 60 percent of those entitled to vote in the proposed new region had to vote for its creation in a plebiscite.[82]

Given the context of Nigerian political realities at this time, co-operation between the NPC and the NCNC, could procure the creation of the state to the exclusion of the

---
82. Ibid., p. 128.

Action Group. Moreover, the synonymity of the three political parties with each of the three regions further meant that co-operation between the North and the East could render the West impotent in such an exercise.[83] There was, however, the question of the plebiscite (referendum), with which the Action Group was in a position to successfully play an obstructive role, granted that voters would toe party lines, as suggested by its strength in the 1960 election.

As if the Mid-West region was pre-ordained to be created, an intra-party conflict erupted within the leadership cadre of the Action Group in the West - a situation which was adequately capitalized upon by the NCNC. The 1962 Action Group crisis (which will be discussed later) had deteriorated to such a level that the Premier of the West, Chief S.L. Akintola, had to form a new party, the UPP (United People's Party), which relied on the support of the NCNC parliamentarians for the control of the Western legislature. It was to the tune of this new political development that Chief Akintola personally led a high-powered campaign team to canvass openly for the creation of the Mid-West state, as the Premier was quoted to have said, "no party has done more within the last 12 months to make possible the realisation of a Mid-West state than the UPP."[84]

The Mid-West region came into reality when, on Thursday, July 18, 1963, a final result of the referendum showed an average of 75.6 percent in favour of the new region. The creation of the region appeared to be a matter

---

83. Babalola Cole, "The Military Government of Nigeria: Preparation for Democracy", *Short Essays in Political Science Vol. IX,* 1982, p. 1.
84. *Daily Times,* 10 July 1963, p. 3.

supported by all political parties, as Chief Awolowo, leader of the Action Group, was said to have also instructed his party supporters in the area to vote 'Yes.'[85] The realisation that the agitation for the creation of the region was the choice of the people, and that any antagonism towards this objective could be politically unrewarding, might have compelled concession from parties which otherwise would have opposed it.

The Action Group Crisis of 1962

The 1962 conflict which fractionalised the Action Group is considered significant for three reasons: First, it was an important 'remote' cause of military intervention in Nigerian politics. Second, it revealed both the ideological contradictions within the AG, and the emergent 'ideological' distinctions that would continue to demarcate the party from other major parties. (By ideological distinctions, it is the view of this writer that, if ideology is measured by the consistency with which certain programmes are adhered to,[86] the AG and its future protrusion merits the tag 'ideological'). Third, the 1962 crisis is a sine qua non for an understanding of the historical root of post-military realignment in the states making up the former Western region.

Many factors were responsible for the personality conflict between Chief Awolowo and Chief Akintola, but according to John P. Mackintosh, "the original source of conflict lay in Chief Awolowo's surrender of the Premiership of the West and failure to become Federal Prime Minister

---

85. Ojiako, *Nigeria: Yesterday, Today, and ...*, p. 164.
86. Richard S. Katz, *A Theory of Parties and Electoral Systems* (Baltimore and London: The Johns Hopkins University press, 1980), p. 41.

after the Federal election of 1959."[87] The position of Opposition Leader, which became the lot of Chief Awolowo at the federal level, meant that he had no influence and patronage at his disposal, compared with his previous position of Premier. To compensate for this 'loss', Chief Awolowo insisted that, as leader of the party, he should be consulted on the political governance of the West. This attempt at usurpation of power would appear to have been unacceptable to Chief Akintola, who, under the terms of Chief Awolowo, might not have been able to make independent decisions, especially with his counterparts, without a deep consideration of the Awolowo factor. The subsequent 'unilateral' actions taken by Chief Akintola on political issues of expediency, such as the reduction of tax, cocoa prices, and the increment in school fees, coupled with his determination to exert control over political appointments, were sufficient grounds for hostility between the two party leaders. The increment in school fees and, consequently, a reduction in government subsidies to education, were considered a contradiction of party policy, and the Action Group press was quick to launch an attack on Chief Akintola for this.[88]

Ideological "Filtration' in the Action Group

The prominent Nigerian scholar, Kalu Ezera, considers two issues as major causes of the Action Group crisis: the wish of Chief Akintola that the Action Group join a National Government, and the adoption of 'democratic socialism' as

---

87. John P. Mackintosh, *Nigerian Government and Politics* (Evanston: Northwestern University Press, 1966), p. 441.
88. Ibid., p. 442.

a party programme by the leadership of the party.[89]

It was the opinion of Chief S.L. Akintola that the West was suffering because of the Action Group's exclusion from the Federal coalition. If the AG were part of the coalition, the danger of creating the Mid-Western state out of the West could be averted, and the threat of extending the Federal Territory to the South, and possibly taking a part of Oyo Province to the North would not have been contemplated. In short, Chief Akintola seemed to be considering the interest of the Yorubas within the national context, and was of the opinion that the politics of confrontation at the centre was not rewarding. Joining the coalition would mean that party competition would be traded for political sensitivity, as the three major parties would not want to offend each other. This approach would further mean that minority group interests, which, at this time, were being championed by the Action Group, would be left to suffer. It was not surprising that Chief Awolowo received support from party leaders in the East and North, who believed that "the party should go on pressing for democracy and minority rights, hoping that one day they would triumph."[90]

The conflict between Chiefs Awolowo and Akintola finally came into the open during the party's convention at Jos in January 1962. It became clear at this convention that the rift was not only between two personalities, but also between two different 'ideological' centres within the AG. Chief Awolowo had, since 1960, attempted to transform

---

89. Kalu Ezera, *Constitutional Developments in Nigeria,* 2nd ed. (Cambridge: Cambridge University Press, 1964), pp. 270-271.

90. Mackintosh, *Nigerian Government and Politics,* p. 43.

the Action Group into a national party by attracting the support of the Nigerian youth, with a programme of 'democratic socialism.' This programme, which emphasised the equal enjoyment of social amenities, further buttressed the determination of Awolowo's faction of the A.G. to not join the National Government, which, at this time, had come to be regarded as comprised of "bourgeois aristocrats and selfish middle classes".[91] The new policy approach heralded an ideological "battle between the young radicals led by Awolowo and the businessmen and traditional rulers led by Chief Akintola."[92] 'Democratic socialism' was rationalised by Awolowo's contention that:

> *there is a growing disaffection between the privileged and non privileged classes (so-called) within the party. If this disaffection has not yet ripened into open hostility, it is because those who regard themselves as non privileged are still hoping that their chance will not be too long in coming, either by the displacement of those who are actually, or are suspected of, enjoying party patronage, or by the creation of more privileges.*[93]

Chief Akintola seemed not to subscribe to a policy of 'democratic socialism', and, in fact, he merely regarded the programme "as the work of revolutionary babes who haven't the political astuteness to gain the party a single vote."[94] The ambition to expand was considered by Chief Akintola, in the realities of Nigerian politics, unrealistic,

---

91. Ojiako, *Nigeria: Yesterday, Today, and...*, p. 96.
92. Ojiako, *Nigeria: Yesterday, Today, and...*, p. 96.
93. Ibid., p. 97.
94. Ibid., p. 96.

and he therefore preferred that the AG should join the Federal coalition, and remain in the West.

The highlight of the Jos convention was that ideological contradictions in the AG were revealed. The beginning of the 'filtration' began when "Chiefs Akintola, Rosiji, Adeyi, and other members of the Western Government walked out."[95] Chief Rosiji was replaced as general secretary of the party by Mr Sam Ikoku.[96]

These events later culminated in a vote of no confidence in Chief Akintola, and his subsequent removal as Premier by the Governor of the West, Oba Adesoji Aderemi, who replaced him with Alhaji Dauda Adegbenro. Akintola refused to 'abdicate', and instead, requested that the Governor convene the House to debate a "motion of confidence in him".[97] On the refusal of the Governor, Chief Akintola asked the Prime Minister, Sir Tafawa Balewa, to revoke the Governor's appointment.

An attempt to confirm the appointment of Alhaji Dauda Adegbenro in the Western House on 25 May led to a riotous confrontation between the two factions of the House, in which the mace, tables, and chairs became fighting instruments. The police were brought in to restore order. The Federal Parliament met on 29 May, 1962 to discuss the Western situation. A state of emergency was declared, and a care-taker committee was appointed to administer the West for six months.

Support for the Akintola faction was immediately issued by the Premiers of Northern and Eastern Nigeria. The Premier

---

95. *West Africa*, 19 May 1962, p. 550.
96. Ibid., p. 550.
97. John P. Mackintosh, *Nigerian Government and Politics*, p. 447.

of the East, Dr Michael Okpara, stressed that the allegation made by Chief Akintola, that E6.5m of Western Government funds had been diverted to a public company, would need to be investigated by a commission.[98]

The decision of the Federal Government to declare a state of emergency on the West was considered an inimical attempt to destroy the AG. The Federal Government's action was considered a usurpation of the power of the courts. Olusanya Awotesu, secretary to the London branch of the Action Group, expressed these bitter views:

> ...the Federal Government has not acted in good faith. The unprecedented and unjustified step taken has not only exposed the predilections and prejudices of the Prime Minister and his collaborators but has also betrayed their conspiracy to destroy the Action Group (whose growing strength has been a cause of embarrassment to them) and the Western Region, the wealthiest in the Federation. The vituperations of the Sardauna of Sokoto and Dr. Okpara since the crisis started support this submission.[99]

UPP – NCNC Alliance in the West

The emergency imposed on the West ended after six months, and in January 1963, Chief S. L. Akintola was asked to resume his position as Premier.

Chief Akintola, together with his parliamentary supporters, had formed a new party, the United People's Party (UPP), which received the sympathy of the NCNC

---

98. *West Africa*, 2 June 1962, p. 607.
99. *West Africa*, 9 June 1962, p. 630.

leadership - a sympathy which, consequently, was translated into an alliance between the UPP and the NCNC in the West.

Meanwhile, allegations of corruption and treason had been brought against Chief Awolowo and some top members of the Action Group. It was alleged that Awolowo had plotted to overthrow the Federal Government, to establish a more 'progressive' administration. He was found guilty by the court, and was jailed along with his convicted co-plotters. The imprisonment of Awolowo did not, in any way, diminish criticism that the Federal Government was corrupt and conservative.

In the West, efforts continued to be made, especially by traditional rulers, to reunify the two factions of the Action Group, the AG and the UPP. The climax of the efforts was the announcement made on July 1, 1963, that both the UPP and the AG had resolved to come together "and collaborate in order to usher in an era of unity, peace, tranquillity, progress and welfare of all people throughout the Region."[100]

It became headline news that Akintola and Adegbenro had embraced one another. While a 'three-party' government was being contemplated by the UPP and the AG, the NCNC central working committee considered Akintola's pact with the AG as a "clandestine act" and "a blow on mutual trust" on the grounds that the NCNC partner was not consulted.[101] The attempt at re-uniting the UPP and the AG did not work after all, and the UPP/NCNC coalition continued to govern the West.

---

100. *Daily Times*, 2 July 1963, p. 1.
101. Ibid., 4 July 1983, p. 1.

N.P.C./N.C.N.C. in Crisis

The Federal Government coalition was not an easy one. The more educated NCNC members had expected to be dominant "in spite of the numerical superiority of the NPC."[102] Contrary to this expectation, the NPC men "proved extremely able politicians," and asserted themselves as de facto leaders of the alliance.[103] The NCNC members were, therefore, becoming disillusioned with the partnership.

It was clear to the NCNC that the numerical advantage of the NPC, based on the population of the North, was the basis for the latter's dominance in national politics. National census was due late in 1963, and it was the expectation of Southerners that results would prove that "the North in reality had a smaller population than the South."[104] With the NCNC in control of the East, Mid-West, and proving strong competition in the West, the rulership of the nation under a NCNC government was considered only a matter of time. All these mathematical speculations became null, however, as the census results proved that the population of the North was larger than the South.[105] There were charges that the statistics had been manipulated, with cows, goats, and domestic pets counted as part of the human population. Frustration over political

---

102. S. A. Akintoye, *Emergent African States,* p. 140.
103. Ibid., p. 140.
104. Ibid., p. 140.
105. Ibid., p. 140.

Simultaneous with events at the national level, was the faltering UPP/NCNC relationship in the West. The sympathy of Chief Akintola's UPP for the NPC was unhidden, and the UPP was becoming a precursor of NPC expansion to the Western flank of the South. Chief Akintola was friendly with the Prime Minister, Sir Tafawa Balewa, and with the Premier of the North, Sir Ahmadu Bello – both NPC leaders. Chief Akintola, as a political realist, saw that the national 'cake', as it were, was more on the NPC's plate than the NCNC's. It should, therefore, not be a surprise that when the NPC/NCNC coalition was cracking at the early part of 1964, the UPP/ NCNC alliance was also falling apart in the West. Meanwhile, Chief Akintola had succeeded in wooing many NCNC leaders in the West to join forces with him to form a brand new party; the Nigerian National Democratic Party (NNDP). The eventual formation of the party, with the acquiescence of influential Yoruba-born NCNC leaders, began the erosion of NCNC influence in the West.

The 1964 Federal Election: The Emergence of Two National Alliances

The 1964 Federal election was fought in what appeared to be a two-party battle. The crack in the Federal coalition, and the various party conflicts in the West, had culminated in the emergence of new alliances. The NPC and the NNDP aligned to form the Nigerian National Alliance (NNA), while the NCNC and the AG teamed together to form the United Progressive Grand Alliance (UPGA).

The alliance between the NCNC and the AG was strengthened by mutual distrust for the 1963 census. Owing to the crisis which had weakened the Action Group, it now seemed that NCNC leadership was indisputable. With Awolowo in jail, and with no matching political figure in the AG to compete with the Premier of the East, Dr Michael Okpara became the natural leader of the UPGA. The terms of the alliance were clear: "...in a republican Nigeria there should be an Executive President, a post which could be held by the NCNC while the Action Group should be offered the post of the Prime Minister."[106]

The 1964 campaigns were rough and riotous. At the governmental level, the NNDP was in control of the West, but whether or not it had won the hearts and support of the masses remained to be seen. The 1964 election would provide the first test. The release of the popular Chief Awolowo from jail was the strategy which the UPGA was relying on and emphasising in the West. The NPC was accused of being "a feudalistic and ultra-conservative party," while the NPC claimed to have made some progress for Nigeria.[107]

Although the highly disputed 1963 census had projected a population change from 36,000,000 in 1953 to 55,000,000, the number of seats in the House remained at 312. The number of seats allocated per region was altered from the 1959 allocations to meet the new changes. The North dropped from 174 to 167, although it had claimed a population increase; the East also dropped from 73 to 70; the Western Region, which then included the Mid-West area, had 62 seats in 1959, but in 1964 its share was reduced to 57 seats; the new Mid-Western Region had 14,

---

106. *Daily Times,* 23 November 1962, p. 2.
107. Richard Harris, "Nigeria: Crisis and Compromise," *Africa Report,* March 1965, p. 27.

while the Federal Territory of Lagos had its seats increased from 3 to 4.[108]

The highlight of the election was the UPGA's allegation of rigging planned by the NNA, causing a boycott of the election to be ordered, especially in the East. The Premier of the Mid-Western-controlled NCNC, Chief Dennis Osadebay, encouraged the people of the new region to vote; whatever victory was recorded in the region for UPGA represented NCNC strength. The following table shows the results of the election.[109]

Region	Allocated Seats	NNA	UPGA	Indep.	Seat Unfilled (No Polling)
North	167	162	4	1	0
East	70	0	19	0	51
West	57	38	18	1	0
Mid-West	14	0	13	0	(unreported)
Lagos	4	0	0	1	3
	312	**200**	**54**	**3**	**54**

---

108. Richard Harris, Africa Report, p. 26.
109. Ibid., p. 30.

The Third Post-Electoral Coalition

It was clear from the boycott that the nation was heading for a major crisis. It was difficult for Dr Nnamdi Azikiwe, who, as a result of the republican constitution of 1963, had become President, to call on the NNA leader, Sir Tafawa Balewa, to form a government despite the 'victory' claimed by his party. After much deliberation, crisis was averted, and a broad-based national government was formed, sequel to the completion of elections in areas where the election was boycotted. A mammoth cabinet of 54 ministers was formed. The NPC had 22 members, 15 of which were of cabinet rank. The NCNC and the NNDP were assigned 16 and 14 seats respectively (11 NCNC and 7 NNDP were of cabinet rank).[110] It is worth noting that the so-called broad-based government was formed to the exclusion of the Action Group.

The 1965 Election In The West

The dominance of the NPC continued to wax stronger and stronger in the North, while the NCNC now controlled two regions: the East and the Mid-West. There was a government in the West, the popularity of which remained to be tested.

The 1965 elections to the Western legislature is remarkable in the annals of Nigerian history. It was a mockery of democracy, and it was in fact the final straw that broke the back of democracy and paved the way for 13 years of military rule.

---

110. Schwarz, Jr., *Nigeria: The Tribes, The Nation, or The Race*, p. 147.

The NNDP was determined to maintain its hold, whether it was popular or not. It was an open secret that party elites were prepared to rig the elections.

Electoral malpractices were at their peak. Many NNDP candidates were declared to have won unopposed, without giving their opponents the chance to register. Victories were announced one day, denied the next, and vice versa. The NNDP's claimed victory was rationalised in the context of past practices; Chief S. L. Akintola admitted in an interview that previous governments in Nigeria had not been defeated in any election.[111]

The astonishing victory of the NNDP precipitated a crisis in which political opponents were slaughtered and their houses burnt. It became apparent that with the masses determined not to accept an unpopular government, the NNDP could not impose itself. There was, however, a proposal by some eminent Nigerians that a compromise be reached, whereby a broad-based government could be formed, but the unpopular NNDP stubbornly refused the participation of UPGA members in its government. The Prime Minister appeared to favour this attempt to compromise, but his will to act was incapacitated by the preference of his party boss,[112] the Sardauna of Sokoto, who seemed to be enjoying the same illusion as his ally, Chief Akintola, that the crisis was a temporary expression and would soon be suppressed.

The devastating and deteriorating crisis in the West was calmed when, in a nationwide coup on January 15, 1966, the military intervened, and sacked all civilian governments.

---

111. *Daily Times,* 12 November 1965, p. 9.
112. Arikpo, *Development of Modern Nigeria,* p. 150.

CHAPTER FOUR

THE MILITARY INTERLUDE AND EVENTS OF CONSEQUENCE TO THE PARTY SYSTEM, 1966-1979

The successful intervention of the military in January 15, 1966 led to a termination of political party activities. The apparent failure of politicians to live up to the standards of civility, as required of a democratic system, paved the way for the military, whose entry was heralded by the Nigerian people as an expression of their disillusionment.

There was, however, disenchantment as to the pattern of the coup led by Major Kaduna Nzeogwu, which, in its execution, gave the impression that the coup was an Ibo attempt to kill prominent politicians from other ethnic groups, especially the North. This was an impression which one of the original planners of the coup, Major Adewale Ademoyega, tried to avoid:

> *Contrary to the load of wicked propaganda that has since been heaped upon us, there was no decision at our meeting to single out any particular ethnic group*

> *for elimination or destruction. Our intentions were honourable, our views were national and our goals were idealistic. We intended that the coup should be national in execution so that it would receive nationwide acclamation.*[113]

Despite this defence, it is difficult to exonerate the planners. The elimination of Sir Tafawa Balewa and Sir Ahmadu Bello, both of whom were Northern leaders, and the violent assassination of Chiefs Akintola and F.S. Okotie-Eboh, from the West and the Mid-West respectively, with the seemingly refusal of the coup planners to extend the 'cleaning exercise' to Eastern Nigeria, suggest some elements of prejudice within the nobility of this plot.

The ideas of the young officers who planned the coup received no opportunity to be tested. Following the tradition of military hierarchy, Major General J.T.U. Aguiyi-Ironsi (an Ibo), who had probably not anticipated a coup, saw himself as Head of State and Government of Nigeria. He soon became unpopular with Northerners because of his much-resented 'Decree No. 34' of 24 May, 1966, establishing a unitary rule. Unitary rule, among many other things, meant that Federal appointments would be based on standardised and uniform criteria. It further meant that the relatively few graduates from the North would face competition "from far larger number[s] of Southern graduates."[114] This resurgence of an erstwhile fear, that the educationally backward North would be subordinate

---

113. Ademoyega, *Why We Struck* (Evans Brothers (Nigeria Publishers) Limited, 1981), p. 60.
114. Irving Leonard Markovitz, *Power and Class in Africa: An Introduction to Change and Conflict in African Politics* (New Jersey: Prentice-Hall, Inc., 1977), pp. 315-316.

to the South seemed to lend credence to the impression that the January 1966 coup was an Ibo plan to dominate Nigeria.

Preceded by killings directed against Ibo residents in the North, the officers and men of Northern origin struck a retaliatory blow, in which many Ibo officers, including Major General Aguiyi Ironsi, were killed. Lieutenant-Colonel Yakubu Gowon, in a fashion undisguisedly demonstrated as a restoration of 'Northern leadership,' took over as Head of State.

Gowon's ascension to power was not an easy one. Tension had developed between the East and the North, and the fact that Gowon's assumption of office was considered a contradiction of military hierarchical tradition brought a challenge to the very basis of his authority. The Military Governor of the East, Lieutenant-Colonel Odumegwu Ojukwu, who claimed to be Gowon's senior, became apprehensive of the latter's sudden climb. The distrust between the East and the North, which was growing each day, culminated in an abortive attempt at secession by the former.

To some extent, Gowon proved to be a successful war administrator, but later incurred the opprobrium of public opinion by his refusal to hand over government to civilians when promised, and also by the overt inclination of his administration towards economic mismanagement.[115] When, eventually, he was ousted in a bloodless coup on 29 July, 1975 (exactly nine years after a coup had installed him), his exit was mourned only by a few people.

Gowon's expulsion brought in a ruthless but dynamic

---

115. *Daily Times*, 31 July 1975, p. 3.

administrator, General Murtala Mohammed. Mohammed's administration was of a relatively short duration, but highly remarkable. Corrupt officials were purged, and governmental programmes were religiously adhered to. After six rather successful months in office, Mohammed was assassinated in an abortive coup. His immediate lieutenant, General Olusegun Obasanjo, stepped into his shoes. With a loyal commitment to a cause, General Obasanjo continued the programs charted by his predecessor. Power was handed over to civilians after a series of elections in 1979.

Having given the above overview of the military administration in Nigeria, the remainder of this chapter will be devoted to several major events that impacted on the origin and development of Nigeria's party system. Included are:

(1) The creation of states,

(2) The civil war, and

(3) The adoption of a presidential constitution patterned after the United States' presidential/ congressional system.

The Creation of States

The creation of states is a significant contribution of the military administration to Nigerian politics. There are two aspects to understanding the importance of this contribution. First, Nigeria emerged as a progressive amalgamation of various 'kingdoms,' each of which had existed as a separate entity. The incompatibility of diverse cultures, coupled with the tendency of larger groups to predominate minor ones, became sufficient cause for agitation by the latter for exclusive units of their own.

Second, the demarcation of Nigeria's regional boundaries had presented a situation whereby one single region was strong enough to dominate others. The Northern region of Nigeria was the dominant unit in Nigeria's regional set-up. This issue could be circumvented by the introduction of a state system.

The Willink Commission of 1958, while making minor regulations, refused to create new states. The British Government was of the opinion that if new states were to be created, the states must be given two years to settle down. Since the nationalists were in haste for independence, the rationale behind the British position could not be realistically considered. It is, however, to the credit of the British that its position has since been exonerated:

> *In (our) common desire to win independence, many vital problems were left unsolved. One of these outstanding problems was the creation of more states which would have provided a more lasting foundation for stability of the Federation of Nigeria. The British Government pointed out at the time that if new states were to be created, the new states must be given at least two years to settle down before independence could be granted. On reflection, Nigerian leaders have admitted that the British were right and they were wrong on this vital issue in hurrying to independence without solving the problem of stability of the Federation.*[116]

---

116. *The Struggle for One Nigeria* (Lagos, Federal Ministry of Information, 1967), p. 3.

Post-independence governments in Nigeria were equally unresponsive to the various demands for the creation of new states. It should be recognised that in the Tiv area of Northern Nigeria, the demand for a Middle-Belt state led to disturbances in 1920, 1939, 1945, 1948, 1960, and 1964[117] — disturbances which were ruthlessly suppressed by the British and, later, the NPC governments. The series of conflicts endemic of the NPC and UMBC leaders in the 1950's and 1960's explain the frustration of the Tiv people.

In the Eastern region, there had been an unsuccessful demand for the creation of a Calabar-Ogoja-Rivers state since the 1940's. The British, as usual, seemed not to favour this. The emergence of an Ibo-dominated NCNC further dampened the hope for the creation of this state. Although the NCNC favoured the creation of states, this was only so long as the East was not the target. It was therefore not unexpected that, when the military took over the government in 1966, and an Ibo leader became Head of State, a situation of frustration and hopelessness developed. In an effort to incorporate the minorities in the East, Isaac Boro, Sam Owonaro, and Nottingham Dick led an attempted secession by an illegal declaration of a "Delta People's Republic."[118]

The West was sensitive about the territory of Lagos and this was expressed at the 1953 Conference, held in London. The feeling of Northern leaders, "that whoever administered Lagos would control, and perhaps deny them,

---

117. Tekena N. Tamuno, "Separatist Agitations in Nigeria Since 1914," *The Journal of Modern African Studies*, 8, 4 (1970), p. 575.
118. Tamuno, *The Journal of Modern African Studies*, p. 577.

their key outlet at Apapa"[119] received the sympathy of the British administrators. While Lagos was transformed into a Federal territory after this conference, demand for its transformation into a state was spear-headed by some local leaders.

In spite of the series of agitations for the creation of states, civilian administrations did not make any meaningful effort. The only state/region created was the Mid-West, which appeared a 'conspiratorial' attempt by the Balewa Government to curtail the growing influence of the 'recalcitrant' A.G. in that area.

The advent of the military provided an opportunity for states to be created without employing the cumbersome guidelines enumerated by the constitution. In fact, the constitution was suspended when the military came in. With the deteriorating relationship between the East and the Federal Government, the creation of states became an instrument through which Ibo strength could be weakened. For a long time, distrust had existed between the Ibos and the minorities in the East; the creation of a COR state was therefore considered an opportunity to secure the loyalty of these minority groups. The irreconcilable conflict, which culminated in a declaration of secession by the East, compelled General Gowon to break down the country into twelve states by decree: 6 in the North, 3 in the East, 1 of the entire Mid-West, the Colony province of the Western region and Lagos States, and the Western region, which remained as it was.[120]

---

119. Ibid., p. 569.
120. *Daily Times,* 28 May 1967, p. 2.

The division of the East into three states was not recognised by the Eastern government, since the entire area had seceded to become the 'Republic of Biafra.' However, the Federal Government was determined to end secession, and at the same time enforce the partition of these states. The Federal Government was able to receive the support of the minorities in the East in its war efforts because of this 'thoughtful' strategy. Adaka Boro, who became the de facto leader of the minorities, enlisted in the national army, and was given the substantive rank of Major.

Additional states were later created by Gowon's successor, General Murtala Mohammed. With a consideration to "bring government near to the people, while at the same time ensuring even development within a federal structure of government,"[121] 7 additional states were created to bring the total number of states to a 19-state structure. The former Northern region consisted of ten states, while the Eastern and Western regions were four and three states respectively; Lagos and the Mid-West remained unchanged.

Subsequent military administrators – General Ibrahim Babangida (August 1985 - August 1993) and General Sani Abacha (November 1993 – June 1998) – created 17 additional states to bring about the present 36-state structure. Abacha went a step further, in demarcating the federation into six geo-political zones.

The Civil War, 1967-1970

The Nigerian civil war was a culmination of many factors, which included: the incompatibility of diverse cultures,

---

121. Ibid., 4 February 1976, p. 3.

unequal educational and social development of the component units, systemic flaws, the uneven partition of regional units, and the politicisation of the military along ethnic lines.

Wars of secession are not uncommon to federal unions, and the fact that Nigeria fought a civil war was not an aberration. The United States fought a civil war to prevent the South from breaking away, while the East Pakistanis succeeded in creating an independent state of Bangladesh out of Pakistan. The failure of 'Biafra' to successfully secede from Nigeria could be explained as due to lack of support for such a cause by the major powers.[122]

Wars often present conditions that are conducive to political realignment. In the case of Nigeria, three factors are considered pertinent to an understanding of post-war realignment: the role of 'Western Nigeria' in the crisis, the behaviour of 'Biafran' troops in war-affected areas, and the spirit of conciliation with which the war was concluded.

The Role of 'Western Nigeria' in the Crisis

The East expected much from the West during the crisis, but would appear to have been disappointed. There was a common feeling of Northern domination of the rest of the country, which, in essence, was a major factor in the alliance between the NCNC and the AG in the 1964 Federal election. The deteriorating political situation in the country was, therefore, considered an opportunity for the South to sever itself from the North.

---

122. Manuel G. Mendoza and Vince Napoli, *Systems of Society An Introduction to Social Science,* 2nd Edition, (Lexington, Massachusetts: D.C. Heath and Company, 1977), p. 432.

The East had the impression that the West was with them. Chief Awolowo, who was the acknowledged leader of the Yorubas at that time, played a mediating role during the crisis. The series of ad hoc meetings to settle the crisis was, however, boycotted by Lieutenant-Colonel Ojukwu, on his belief that he was not safe due to the presence of Northern troops at the proposed venues in either the Mid-West, West, or Lagos. Expressing the mood of the Yorubas, and at the same time, paving the way for a situation whereby Ojukwu would attend meetings, Chief Awolowo requested in a letter to Colonel Adebayo (Governor of the West) that Northern troops in the West and Lagos be removed on the grounds that they "constitute an army of occupation, and that their non-removal has virtually reduced the said territories to the status of a 'protectorate.'"[123] Chief Awolowo, however, pointed out that on the implementation of this recommendation, the refusal of Lieutenant-Colonel Ojukwu to attend future meetings should be viewed as an invitation to having "the rest of the country without exception ranged against himself for deliberately setting out to destroy the federation."[124]

Chief Awolowo, after frustrating attempts at settlement, was not without the impression that Eastern Nigeria was on its way out, and that what "some people with influence in government circles" now wanted was "to help Eastern Nigeria out of Nigeria and form a new federation, on terms which are already cut and dried by them from among the remaining units."[125] This impression was later followed by

---

123. *Daily Times,* 25 April 1967, p. 18.
124. Ibid, p. 18.
125. Ibid., p. 1.

a 'conditional imperative' by Chief Awolowo that "if the Eastern Region is allowed by acts of omission or commission to secede from or opt out of Nigeria, that the Western Region and Lagos must also stay out of the Federation."[126]

Awolowo's condition for the exit of the West was later interpreted to mean that, "if the East goes, the West will follow." When the East eventually seceded and the West did not follow, the Yorubas in general, and Awolowo in particular, were taken as traitors. Chief Awolowo has since tried to explain his stand in a book published on the civil war.[127]

Enmity between the East and the West did not stop on the unfulfilled promise, but grew with Awolowo's conspicuous efforts to end the war. The incursion of the 'Biafran' troops into the Mid-West was followed up with an exhortation on the part of the Yorubas to liberate themselves from the Hausa-Fulani domination. Chief Awolowo, in a broadcast to the Yorubas, encouraged them to "lose no time and spare no efforts in giving every conceivable support to the Federal troops in defence of their homeland, and of the fatherland."[128]

Chief Awolowo, as Commissioner for Finance, took measures which helped to end the war without external borrowing, and at the same time, inflicted much suffering on the rebels. The decisions to change the Nigerian currency and to ban certain food importation into 'Biafra' helped to weaken the morale of the secessionist troops. It is widely believed by 'Biafrans' that the statement, "starvation is a

---

126. Ibid., 2 May 1967, p. 6.
127. Obafemi Awolowo, *Awo on the Nigerian Civil War* (Ikeja, Nigeria: John West Publications Ltd., 1981), pp. i-ix.
128. Ibid., p. 80.

legitimate instrument of war,"[129] credited to Awolowo, is a display of the latter's hostility to the people. The statement has been explained by Chief Awolowo to refer only to soldiers in the war and not to innocent civilians.[130]

Alleged Behaviour of 'Biafran' Troops In War-Affected Areas

The behaviour of 'Biafran' troops in war-affected areas left much to be desired. It was, however, not unexpected that the treatment of the 'minority' groups in the secessionist enclave would not be accommodating. As has been pointed out earlier in this book, there was distrust of Ibos by the minorities; the unenthusiastic approach of the latter to the civil war only intensified the sourness of the existing relationship.

Various atrocities, such as rape and looting of properties, were reportedly committed in this area by the Ibos. A respected journal has explained the post-war estrangement between the Ibos and the 'minority' groups (constituting the peoples of Rivers and Cross-River states) with the civil war: these states suffered badly in the civil war, when Ibo army officers dragooned them into the pseudo-state of 'Biafra'[131]

The Mid-West area presents another interesting case-study of alleged 'Biafran' misbehaviour. The area was somehow compatible with the East and had voted overwhelmingly for the Ibo-dominated N.C.N.C. in the past.

---

129. Awolowo, *Awo on the Nigerian Civil War,* p. iv.
130. Awolowo, *Awo on the Nigerian Civil War,* p. iv.
131. The Most African Country: A Survey of Nigeria." *The Economist,* 23 January 1982, page unknown.

The Governor of the State, Brigadier Ejoor, had taken a position, which in a disciplined and unified army should have been viewed as treachery and disloyalty. He had made consistent remarks that he would not allow Federal troops to be stationed in his state, which was contiguous to 'Biafra,' in order not to turn the place into a battleground. It was in the light of the Federal Government's acquiescence to this position that a successful invasion of the Mid-West by 'Biafran' troops was made possible. Brigadier Ejoor later claimed that he had escaped on a bicycle.[132]

The Mid-West state was immediately proclaimed an independent and sovereign 'Republic of Benin.' The 'Biafran' troops claimed to have come in to liberate the area from Hausa-Fulani domination. If liberation was intended, the behaviour of 'Biafran' troops did not demonstrate it. An eyewitness account has attributed the Mid-Westerners' unwillingness to welcome the troops as members of 'Eastern Nigeria,' known to Mid-Westerners as partners in the days of party politics, to this indiscipline. 'Biafrans' did not come "to continue the political struggle of old,"[133] rather, they came in as foreigners and plunderers:

> *They behaved like an army of occupation, by molesting the people. These problems could have been solved if only the units had their complement of officers or something near it, not in this reverse case where a whole battalion had only one or two seasoned officers. When the Oba of Benin, Akenzua II and his chiefs summoned me to one of their*

---

132. General Olusegun Obasanjo, *My Command: An Account of the Nigerian Civil War, 1967-70* (London: Heineman Educational Books Ltd., 1981), p. 37.
133. Ademoyega, *Why We Struck*, p. 165.

> *meetings, they did not discuss how the liberation of the Mid West could be made a reality. They simply wanted the menace of the Biafran troops removed...*[134]

Gowon's Policy of "No Victor, No Vanquished"

The magnanimity with which General Yakubu Gowon concluded the war is worth mentioning. The fact that he viewed the war as mere fratricidal feuding which needed not be punished with executions was sufficient signal to Ibos that they were not unwanted in a united Nigeria. The story of the amnesty becomes more interesting when one ponders the fact that Gowon was a Northerner, and, contrary to the expectations of outsiders, victory was not used as an opportunity to silence the intransigence of Ibos.

Pope Paul VI appeared somehow doubtful of the capability of the Federal Government to display magnanimity by granting amnesty[135] to the predominantly Catholic 'Biafrans', but later events proved him wrong. Gowon was responsive to international opinion, and proved with dignity that the civil war was not a war of genocide, but a baptism of fire not uncommon with federal unions. Pleas were made by the Prime Minister of Britain, Mr Harold Wilson; the President of France, Georges Pompidou; and Mr Elliot Richardson, on behalf of the U.S.[136] Gowon followed his promise of no 'Nuremberg trials' with a program of reconstruction, reconciliation, and rehabilitation.

---

134. Ibid., p. 165.
135. Peter Schwab, *Biafra* (New York: Facts on File, Inc., 1971), p. 125.
136. Ibid., p. 129.

The Adoption of a Presidential Constitution

The adoption of a presidential constitution, patterned after the United States' presidential/congressional system, is considered by this writer as a great legacy of the military administration to Nigerian politics. The intent of the constitution as a document, to usher in a "unifying political process", was stated by General Olusegun Obasanjo in a broadcast to the nation on 1 October, 1976.[137] The new constitution was a complete divorce from the British parliamentary type, which, in the ethnological context of Nigeria, only proved divisive. Certain features of the new constitution need to be identified for their relevance to this study: the election of the president and the establishment of political parties.

Chapter VI, Sections 125 and 126, establishes the conditions under which a candidate may win an election to the Office of President:[138]

125. *A candidate for an election to the Office of President shall be deemed to have been duly elected to such office where, being the only candidate nominated for the election —*

> *(a) he has a majority of Yes votes over No votes cast at the election; and*

---

137. Oyeleye Oyediran, ed., *Survey of Nigerian Affairs,* 1976-1977 (Lagos: Nigerian Institute of International Affairs, 1981), p. 125.
138. *The Constitution of the Federal Republic of Nigeria 1979* (Lagos: Department of Information, Printing Division, Reproduced by the Government Printer, Governor's Office, Printing Division, Benin City, Bendel State, Nigeria, 1981), pp. 41-42.
   *Not mentioned in the constitution.

(b) he has not less than one quarter of the votes cast at the election in each of at least two-thirds of all the states in the federation, but where the only candidate fails to be elected in accordance with this section, then there shall be fresh nominations.

126. *(1) A candidate for an election to the office of President shall be deemed to have been duly elected where, there being more than 2 candidates for the election; and*

   (a) he has the highest number of votes cast at the election; and

   (b) he has not less than one quarter of the votes cast at the election in each of at least two-thirds of all the States in the Federation.

   (2) In default of a candidate duly elected in accordance with subsection (2) of this section there shall be a second election in accordance with subsection (4) of this section at which the only candidates shall be –

   (a) the candidate who scored the highest number of votes at any election held in accordance with the said subsection (2) of this section: and

   (b) one among the remaining candidates who has a majority of votes in the highest number of States, so however that where there are more than one candidate with a majority of votes in the highest number of States, the candidate with the highest total of votes cast at the election shall be the second candidate election.

(3) In default of a candidate duly elected under the foregoing subsections, the Federal Electoral Commission shall within 7 days of the result of the election held under the said sub sections, arrange for an election between the two candidates and a candidate at such election shall be deemed to have been duly elected to the office of President if –

> *(a) he has a majority of the votes cast at the election; and*
>
> *(b) he has not less than one-quarter of the votes cast at the election in each of at least two-thirds of all the States in the Federation.*

(4) In default of a candidate duly elected under subsection (4) of this section, the Federal Electoral Commission shall within 7 days of the result of the election held under the aforesaid subsection (4), arrange for another election between the two candidates to which the subsection relates and a candidate at such election shall be deemed to have been duly elected to the office of President if he has a majority of the votes cast at the election.

Chapter VI, Section 202 stipulates the restriction on formation of political parties:[139]

202. No association by whatever name called shall function as a political party, unless –

> *(a) the names and addresses of its national officers are registered with the Federal Commission;*
>
> *(b) the membership of the association is open to every*

---

139. *The Constitution of the Federal Republic of Nigeria 1979*, p. 65.

citizen of Nigeria irrespective of his place of origin, sex, religion or ethnic grouping;

(c) a copy of its constitution is registered in the principal office of the Commission in such form as may be prescribed by the Commission;

(d) any alteration in its registered constitution is also registered in the principal office of the Commission within 30 days of the making of such alteration;

(e) the name of the association, its emblem or motto does not contain any ethnic or religious connotation or give the appearance that the activities of the association are confined to a part only of the geographical area of Nigeria; and

(f) the headquarters of the association is situated in the capital of the Federation.

*It must have established branch offices in at least two-thirds (i.e., 13) of the States, and its organisation must effectively penetrate into the local government areas.[140]

---

140. Dr. William D. Graf, *Elections 1979: The Nigerian Citizens' Guide to Parties, Politics, Leaders and Issues* (Lagos: A *Daily Times* Publication), p. 59.

Both the constitutional requirements for the election of the President and the establishment of political parties are complementary in many respects. They are attempts at eliminating ethnic politics symptomatic of the pre-military era. Under the parliamentary system, it was a convenient practice for the NPC, endowed with sufficient political support in the North, to rely on one of the political parties in the South for a post-electoral coalition government. Under the new constitution, the need for a party to court the entire national constituency has become paramount, if such a party is to have any serious claim to the presidency.

Moreover, the establishment of a national constituency for the President, with its 'winner-take-all' character, has established the office as the most important target, which any political party must scramble to achieve.

CHAPTER FIVE

POST-MILITARY PARTY POLITICS, 1979 TO 1983: THE SCRAMBLE FOR THE PRESIDENCY

In its commitment to transfer power to civilians, the military administration lifted its ban on political party activities in September 1978.[141] The anxiety of politicians to return to power was expressed in the speed with which the formation of political parties was announced. Within 24 hours, the emergence of the first party was announced, and by December 18, the number of 'parties' had increased to 53.[142]

It should be recalled that a political party, in order to merit registration, was required to have established its "branch offices in at least two-thirds of the states, and its organization penetrate into local government areas."[143] The

---

141. Graf, *Elections 1979,* p. 54.
142. Ibid., p. 54.
143. Chapter VI, Section 125(b), *The Constitution of the Federal Republic of Nigeria 1979.*

Federal Electoral Commission's (FEDECO) adherence to this guideline explains why only 5 of the 19 'political parties' that had felt prepared to register were recognised. These five political parties were:

1. The National Party of Nigeria (NPN), whose leader was Alhaji Shehu Shagari
2. The Nigerian People's Party (NPP), led by Dr Nnamdi Azikiwe
3. The Peoples Redemption Party (PRP), under Alhaji Aminu Kano
4. The Great Nigerian People's Party (GNPP), with Alhaji Waziri Ibrahim at its head, and
5. The Unity Party of Nigeria (UPN), headed by Chief Obafemi Awolowo.[144]

The campaigns for the 1979 election were remarkable. Except for the UPN and the NPP, whose leaders were based in the old Western and Eastern regions respectively, the other three political leaders were from the North. The constitutional requirement which stated that in order to win the presidency, a candidate must secure the highest number of votes, and also win at least one-fourth of the votes in two-thirds of the states, became sufficient cause to compel political leaders from the North, who, in the pre-military era, had confined themselves to that region, to campaign in the South. Moreover, the concentration of three political parties seemed to have fractionalised the heretofore monolithic North, so that the need to count on Southern votes became almost inevitable.

---

144. Ibid., p. 58.

The elections scheduled for July and August 1979 were contested in five consecutive stages: the House of Senate, the House of Representatives, the State House of Assembly, the gubernatorial election, and the presidential election. The pattern of election results lends support to the popular assertion that, except for the brand new GNPP, the registered political parties were a mere regrouping of pre-military loyalties. It is therefore considered crucial for the fluency of this study to recognise the correlations as revealed by Professor Whitaker, Jr.: NPC/NPN; AG/UPN; NEPU/PRP; NCNC/NPP.[145] Dr Graf also recognises these correlations and, in fact, supports his conviction by pointing to the fact that the presidential candidate of the NPP, Dr Nnamdi Azikiwe, mistakenly referred to his new party as 'NCNC' on more than six instances during the campaigns.[146] Aside from Alhaji Shehu Shagari, who probably became party leader only because of the assassination of Alhajis Tafawa Balewa and Ahmadu Bello in the January 1966 coup, the other three party leaders had headed the defunct parties correlated with their new ones. Although there are evidences of post-military realignment, party leaders still maintained a strong hold on their core bases.

The Presidential Election

The presidential election is the main focus of this analysis because of its all-encompassing nature. It is the single election that has transformed the nation into one constituency. The fact that the institution of the Presidency

---

145. C.S. Whitaker, Jr., "Second Beginnings: The New Political Framework," *Issue*, XI, Spring/Summer 1981, p. 8.
146. Graf, *Elections 1979*, p. 72.

symbolises national power has made its attainment a major preoccupation of the political parties. The constitution recognises this importance, and has therefore instituted guidelines to ensure that whoever occupies the office must have national acceptance.

The sequential nature of the elections revealed the strength of the political parties, and therefore, gave room for projections. It became almost clear, after the first three elections, that although the NPN was meeting the requirements with consistency in 12 states, nevertheless, a run-off election would be the deciding factor, since 13 was construed to mean two-thirds of 19 states. This situation led to panicking among the presidential candidates of the NPN and the UPN, which had now emerged as the two major contestants, thereby creating an obsession for cooperation from the minor political parties.

The pattern of electoral results was consistent throughout the elections. There was, however, an 'anomalous' result in the gubernatorial election. An alliance of four parties had been summoned, with a motive of stopping the NPN's winning spree. This alliance of 'progressive' forces (which will be discussed later) seemed to have taken off. Chief Obafemi Awolowo, leader of the UPN, realistically based his calculations on the trend of results and, therefore, ordered political parties under the umbrella of the 'progressives,' to vote for one common candidate, where each of the parties (UPN, NPP, GNPP, and PRP) had demonstrated the highest strength.[147] The formula worked, where it was given publicity. It was in the

---

147. *Daily Times,* 25 July 1979, p. 1.

light of these directives that a P.R.P. governor won the election in Kaduna state, thereby creating a situation whereby the Executive had to face a hostile House, dominated by the NPN. The governor, Alhaji Balarabe Musa, was later impeached, partly because Nigerian politicians had not digested the complexities of a political system where such an occurrence can and must be accepted. Balarabe's situation was unusual in a parliamentary system into which Nigerian politicians had been socialised.

It should be noted that the magic of cooperation, which had produced Balarabe Musa, did not receive the support of other presidential candidates, each of whom was expecting a last minute surprise. Hence, the 'progressives' could not agree to direct their votes to a common presidential candidate and thereby paved the way for the NPN's convenient lead. As the table below reveals, Alhaji Shehu Shagari of the NPN satisfied the electoral requirements in 12 states, while also scoring 19.94 percent of the votes in Kano state. The question which immediately arose was: what is the interpretation of two thirds of 19 states?

1979 Presidential Balloting by States

State	Total Votes Cast	Waziri (GNPP) 90(%)	Awolowo (UPN) (%)	Shagari (NPN) (%)	Kano (PRP) (%)	Azikiwe (NPP) (%)
Anambra	1,209,038	1.67	0.75	13.50	1.20	82.88
Bauchi	998,683	16.44	3.00	62.48	14.34	4.74
Bendel	669,511	1.20	53.20	36.20	0.70	8.60
Benue	538,879	7.97	2.57	76.38	1.35	11.77
Borno	710,968	54.04	3.35	34.71	6.52	1.35
Cross Rivers	661,103	15.14	11.76	64.40	1.01	7.66
Gongola	639,138	34.09	21.67	35.52	4.34	4.35
Imo	1,153,355	3.00	0.64	8.80	0.89	84.69
Kaduna	1,382,712	14.00	7.00	43.00	31.00	5.00
Kano	1,195,136	1.54	1.23	19.94	76.41	0.91
Kwara	354,605	5.71	37.48	53.62	0.67	0.52
Lagos	828,414	0.48	83.30	7.18	0.47	9.57
Niger	383,347	16.60	3.67	74.83	3.77	1.11
Ogun	744,668	0.53	92.61	6.23	9.31	0.32
Ondo	1,384,788	0.26	94.50	4.19	0.18	0.86
Oyo	1,396,547	0.57	85.78	12.75	0.32	0.55
Plateau	548,405	6.82	5.29	34.73	3.98	49.70
Rivers	687,951	2.18	10.33	72.65	0.46	14.35
Sokoto	1,348,597	26.61	2.52	66.58	3.33	0.92
Total	**16.846,633**	**10.01**	**29.18**	**33.77**	**10.28**	**16.75**

Source: Whitaker, Jr., *Issue*

Other presidential candidates, especially Chief Awolowo of the UPN, who had only met the requirements in 6 states, expected a run-off election. Dr Azikiwe of the N.P.P. was aware of the pivotal position of his party, and started seeing himself as the beautiful bride to be courted by the two major parties, should an electoral college decision be called for. It was in the process of this uncertainty, that the legal adviser of the NPN, Chief Richard Akinjide, 'conjured' a controversial solution, in that two-thirds of 19 was 12-2/3 and not 13. His contention was accepted by FEDECO, which later declared Alhaji Shehu Shagari as the winner.

Chief Awolowo was not satisfied with FEDECO's decision, on his belief that:

> *When you take 12 as two-thirds of 19 states, it is a contravention of our law. To also take two thirds of 19 states as anything less than 13 is also to violate the law. It is illegal to fractionalise a state.*[148]

Chief Awolowo took his case to the Presidential Electoral Commission, but his petition did not appear attractive to the members, who dismissed the case "because it lacked merit."[149] The Chief made an appeal to the Supreme Court, but the appeal also met with failure, and Shehu Shagari's nomination was finally ratified.[150]

N.P.C./N.P.N. and N.C.N.C./N.P.P.: Fourth Post-Electoral (Coalition) Accord

President Shehu Shagari's administration took off through an accord with the NPP. There were two sides to this

---

148. *Daily Times,* 7 September 1979, p. 1.
149. Ibid., 11 September 1979, p. 1
150. Ibid., 27 September 1979, p. l.

accord: First, Alhaji Shehu Shagari had made a clarion call for a broad-based government for the purpose of "building a united, peaceful and stable nation."[151] He was of the opinion that an atmosphere of friendship was necessary among all Nigerians, and that all "must come together as a family to solve [Nigeria's] common problems, [...] if the nation must be truly great."[152] Second, Nigeria had just adopted a presidential constitution, but the shadows of the British parliamentary system, with its concomitance of coalition for programmic success, were still around. It was, therefore, not unlikely that President Shehu Shagari had considered the strength of the NPN with those of the other four parties before courting for support.

It was not a surprise to anyone when the NPP agreed to join the accord with the NPN. The NPP had flirted with the party and the UPN when the winner of the presidential election had not been declared and, in fact, matters came to a point whereby a merger was contemplated between the two parties in the course of the elections. It was perhaps because of Dr Azikiwe's gerontocratic notion of leadership that the merger did not take place. In spite of the fact that the electoral trends had presented the N.P.N. presidential candidate as more viable, Dr Azikiwe claimed that he could not be asked to step down for Alhaji Shagari because "it was un-African," to ask "an elder to stoop for a younger opponent."[153] When Azikiwe's party eventually gained its place in Nigeria's political demarcation, an NPN/NPP accord

---

151. *Daily Times,* 18 August 1979, p. 1.
152. Ibid., 18 August 1979, p. 1.
153. Ibid., 18 August 1979, p. 1.

redolent of the NPC/NCNC coalition in the pre-military era was consummated "without conditions."[154] If President Shagari saw Dr Azikiwe as unpredictable,[155] the latter's tendency to seize the opportunity of events for political advantage may well justify this impression. Dr Azikiwe gained a reputation for brilliancy, not only in political theory, but also in its practice.

It should, however, be noted that the NPN/NPP accord lasted only 21 months. The NPN leader, Alhaji Shehu Shagari, explained the failure of the accord in an exclusive interview:

> ...The N.P.P. leaders thought that an accord was basically an arrangement for sharing of patronages, for sharing the booty, so to speak, but we did not regard it as such. Our own understanding of the accord was that it provided for co-operation between the two parties in order to help government and get things moving. We found that the N.P.P. was more interested in what it could get out of the accord than really working for the government and the nation. They kept on demanding all sorts of favours and privileges...[156]

Failure of the Accord: What Lessons?

That the NPN/NPP accord was compelled by the need for a smooth passage of executive programmes in the Legislature was further buttressed by Nigeria's Vice President, Dr Alex

---

154. *West Africa,* 17 August 1979, p. 1862.
155. *Africa Now,* November 1982, p. 48.
156. Ibid. p. 48.

Ekwueme.[157] However, the fact that the breakdown of the accord did not call for the dethronement of the Executive provided a lesson in presidential politics.

The capability of the President to convince the Legislature to pass the controversial Economic Stabilisation Temporary Provision Act of 1982, which enabled him to take appropriate measures on the deteriorating economic situations of Nigeria, showed a mastery of presidential power of persuasion and bargaining. An extract from President Shagari's address to a joint session of the National Assembly in April 1982 is revealing:

> ...I have been encouraged from the discussions I have had with your representatives and those held on my behalf...that Nigerians are patriotic enough to realise that now is the time to close ranks to protect the nation...[158]

The contention of Professor Neustadt that the power of the president is the power to persuade and to bargain was clearly demonstrated[159]

As Nigerian politicians might learn from the founding nation of presidential politics (The USA), presidential effectiveness has depended more on a capability to use the attributes of persuasion and bargaining than on relying on a majority of party members in the Legislature, who have their own interests to protect. Instances abound whereby Presidents have gone down in American history as weak despite their parties having the upper hand in the two

---

157. *West Africa,* 17 August 1981, p. 1863.
158. Ibid., 26 April 1982, pp. 113-114.
159. Richard E. Neustadt, Presidential Power: The Politics Of Leadership From FDR To Carter (New York: John Wiley and Sons, Inc., 1980).

Houses, while on the other hand, some Presidents with insignificant party associates in Congress have demonstrated political astuteness in their relationships with the Legislature.

The presidential system of separation of powers demands a different orientation from the parliamentary system, in which a coalition of parties becomes a sine qua non for the survival of government. The term of the Executive is fixed; his appointment may not be terminated without impeachment and conviction. The realisation of this important feature of the presidential system may induce political parties to concentrate efforts on expanding followership, thereby becoming viable contestants for the presidency, rather than relying on post-electoral coalitions for the purpose of sharing political largesse.

Towards a Two-Party System

Readjustment to party politics during, and immediately after, the presidential elections left no observer in doubt as to the changing of Nigerian politics. The withdrawal of the NPP from the accord with the NPN brought the party into a 'renewal' of alliance with other parties. Generally, post-electoral political activities were unprecedented in the annals of Nigerian politics. Reports in connection with party politics dominated Nigeria's major newspapers. Such reports tended to focus on alliances, defections, and the conversion of new entrants. The patterns of these activities seemed to suggest one thing: that Nigeria was moving towards a two-party system.

N.N.A. Versus U.P.G.A. Revisited

In order to appreciate the historical connection of the current trends, there is a need to re-examine the NNA and the UPGA, which emerged in the 1964 election as two national umbrella alliances. A reliable source taxonomised the alliances into their component units.

A. NIGERIAN NATIONAL ALLIANCE (NNA)

- NPC — Northern People's Congress
- NNDP — Nigerian National Democratic Party
- MWDF — Mid-West Democratic Front
- NDC — Niger Delta Congress
- DP — Dynamic Party
- RP — Republican Party
- LSUF — Lagos State United Front

B. UNITED PROGRESSIVE GRAND ALLIANCE (UPGA)

- NCNC — National Convention of Nigerian Citizens
- AG — Action Group
- NEPU — Northern Elements Progressive Union
- UMBC — United Middle Belt Congress[160]

N.N.A./N.P.N.: From Alliance to Fusion

The NNA, of which the nucleus party was the NPC, metamorphosed into the NPN. It is therefore not enough to equate the NPN with the NPC without a due

---

160. Yasphal Tandon and Dilshad Chandarana, ed., *Horizons of African Diplomacy*, (Nairobi: East African Literature Bureau, 1974), p. 242.

consideration of the minor parties that were part of the defunct alliance. In the minority areas of the Eastern region, there had existed the Dynamic Party, and the Niger Delta Congress. In the context of American politics, these associations would be regarded as pressure groups, since they stood more for the single issue of state creation. Nevertheless, their attempt at representation through the electoral process qualifies them as minor parties. With the creation of the Rivers and the Cross River states, these minor parties, albeit insignificant in the pre-military era because of the dominant Ibos in the unit, grew into major forces in their exclusive territories. The distrust of the Ibos,[161] and a reliance on the more predictable force from the North, further unified the people behind the NPN.

The strong position of the NPN in Bendel state (Mid-West) owed its origin to the existence of the Mid-West Democratic Front. This minority party existed as the ally of the NPC; the erosion of the NCNC/NPP base in Bendel, with no less a personality than Chief Dennis Osadebay, former NCNC Premier of the region, throwing his weight behind the NPN, only helped to augment existing loyalty.

In the Western flank of the country, the NPN owed its scant support to the members of the old NNDP.[162] There was no attempt on the part of the old members of the party to regroup in an exclusive political party, and so many of them were assimilated into the umbrella group. The relatively unpopular position of the NPN in this region, compared with the followership of the UPN, reflected the defunct NNDP's unpopularity with the Yorubas, despite

---

161. *The Economist,* 23 January 1982, page unknown.
162. Graf, *Elections 1979,* p. 72.

stubborn efforts to impose itself. With the assassination of Chief Akintola in a military coup, his Deputy Chief Remi Fani-Kayode became the most important link in the historical relationship between the NNDP and the NPC.

The NNA/NPN which seemed to have had no previous influence in the core Ibo area of the East, i.e., Imo and Anambra, made an encouraging entry by taking second position in the five elections. This performance may not be sufficiently explained without a reflection on the civil war, the conclusion of which painted the North as an irreconcilable enemy of the East. There is also the Ibo strategy of joining the predictable winner for political advantages – an objective well-articulated in Chief Odumegwu Ojukwu's declaration for the NPN.[163]

If the NNA/NPN successfully invaded UPGA territory, the Middle-Belt region presents an interesting example of post-military realignment. The UMBC was an important component of the UPGA, and presented a formidable opponent to the defunct NPC in the past. The UMBC was a major advocate of the creation of the Middle-Belt region, a cause which, as noted earlier, led to bloody conflicts over a span of four decades. With the creation of states by the military, it would appear that all the UMBC stood for had been accomplished. The decision of the 'moving spirit' of the party, Mr J.S. Tarka, to align with the N.P.N. explained why the region voted N.P.N. in the 1979 election. Mr Tarka, because of his relentless efforts to create an exclusive territory for the Tivs of the Middle-Belt, was accepted as the "Moses" of his people.[164] Mr Tarka, now dead, is

---

163. *West Africa*, 24 January 1983, p. 232.

considered a venerated founder of the NPN, so that the decision to start the 1983 election campaigns from his place of birth was made to commemorate the memory of this charismatic leader, and first chairman of the party.[165]

However, not everything was a plus for the NPN. The decision of Alhaji Waziri Ibrahim to compete for the national leadership helped to cede a base of the defunct NPC to the then newly-formed GNPP. Waziri Ibrahim's case explains that of the favourite son, who could use available resources to entice his immediate environment, without a capability to win an election in an overall context. Alhaji Waziri Ibrahim was a former minister in the defunct NPC government. He was known to be a shrewd businessman, who had "sold a lot of weapons during the war."[166] His wealth and, consequently, his ambition to become a national leader, spurred him into forming his party, which subsequently disintegrated.[167]

It needs to be highlighted that the NPN, realising that the greater strength of the party was in the North, adopted a formula designed not only to reconvene its allies, but also to entice new entrants. The history of Nigerian leadership seemingly suggests that to be a national leader, one had to be a northerner. The adoption of a zoning formula, which sought to alternate "the geo-ethnic region of (NPN's) presidential and vice-presidential candidates

---

164. Ibid., 3 May 1982, p. 1190.
165. Ibid., 31 January 1983, p. 253.
166. Ray Ekpu, "Waziri: Why are rich men in politics," *Sunday Times*, 16 May 1982, p. 7.
167. Ibid., p. 7.

from one election to the next",¹⁶⁸ was to remove this impression.

Reviving U.P.G.A. – "The 'Progressive Parties' Alliance" (P.P.A.)

If the NNA had transformed without much solicitation, the same was not true with the UPGA. The move towards a UPGA resurgence was compelled only by an NNA/NPN electoral successes. Chief Obafemi Awolowo of the UPN and Alhaji Waziri Ibrahim of the G.N.P.P. were the pioneers of this revival. Although Alhaji Ibrahim was not a part of the defunct UPGA, his somewhat antagonistic position to an N.P.N. victory brought a relatively influential politician into the fold of the 'progressives'.¹⁶⁹ He was consistently with Chief Awolowo throughout the post-electoral protests.

The new alliance was a representation of the UPN, GNPP, NPP, and PRP, although the PRP was initially not an active participant. Reaction to this gang up, as one would rightly expect, was negative on the part of the NPN. The assistant national secretary of the party, Dr Obarogie Ohonbamu, saw the alliance as a concoction of negatives, and therefore concluded that it would not work:

> *Azikiwe's neo-welfarism, plus Awolowo's neo-socialism, plus Waziri's mixed economy, plus Aminu Kano's Marxian socialism equals grand confusion.*¹⁷⁰

---

168. Whitaker, Jr., *Issue*, p. 10.
169. Ojiako, *Nigeria: Yesterday, Today and...*, p. 290.
170. Ibid., p. 292.

The P.R.P. was not without conditions for its entry into the alliance. The national secretary of the party, Mr S.G. Ikoku (who defected into the NPN) gave these conditions:

(1) The identity of the PRP must be preserved;

(2) An agreement to condemn organised electoral malpractices by political parties and agents;

(3) The denunciation of ethnic and religious politics; and

(4) That a government seeking the co-operation of the P.R.P., must be based on a principle of national economic independence.[171]

It should, however, be recalled that the PRP was an immediate beneficiary of the alliance, as Awolowo's directives helped to produce the impeached PRP governor.

With the declaration of the NPN candidate as winner of the presidential election, the alliance received a temporary setback. The NPP saw an opportunity in the NPN's call for an accord, and quickly seized it to benefit from presidential patronages.

While the NPP was in a working accord with the NPN, the UPN became the only major party in the alliance, while the PRP and the GNPP had fractionalised over the issue. The PRP leader, Alhaji Aminu Kano, was insensitive to the alliance, while the two governors of his party were committed participants. The alliance succeeded in creating a council of progressive governors, which had not only

---

171. Ibid., p. 293.

criticised the NPN on certain issues, but had also fostered inter-governmental relationships.

The failure of the NPP to continue with its accord brought the party back into the fold of the 'progressives.' With the AG/UPN, NCNC/NPP, and factions of PRP representing an aspect of the old NEPU, together with a faction of the G.N.P.P. came a resurgence of the old UPGA into a Progressive Parties' Alliance (PPA) – an alliance of political parties united by a perception of the NPN as "the evil of feudalism and ethnic hegemony."[172] The NPN was viewed as a party of the rich. President Shehu Shagari of the NPN, while not refuting the view that the NPN belonged to the rich, humorously retorted that "other parties have rich people too."[173]

P.P.A. – Problem of Fusion

Unlike the NPN, which is a successful example of fusion, the UPGA, which reconvened as the PPA, found it difficult to fuse. The major reason for this setback is partly explained by an inability to compromise on leadership.[174]

It should be noted that the NCNC/NPP, which was the major party in the defunct UPGA, became weaker as a result of post-war realignment. The party lost control of the Mid-West (now Bendel), was denounced in the Rivers and Cross River states, and had its relics consumed by both the UPN and the NPN in the Western flank of the country. It was now a party almost confined to Imo and

---

172. *West Africa,* 3 January 1983, p. 21.
173. *Africa Now,* November 1982, p. 50.
174. A.A. Akinola, "Why Alliances Fail in Nigeria.", *West Africa*, 8 February 19-82, p. 361.

Anambra states, while enjoying a not-too-convenient support in Plateau state.

The AG/UPN, which appeared to be the de facto opponent of the NPN, also lost ground in the East, especially in Imo and Anambra. As the results of the elections indicate, the UPN trailed fifth in these two states. This should be a surprise if one reflects on the fact that this party was the official opposition to the NCNC in that region. Chief Awolowo and his party were denounced because of his failure to lead the West into secession along with Biafra and, moreover, for, his economic measures, which inflicted much suffering on the rebels. However, with the positional advantage of the UPN in the PPA, Chief Awolowo appeared the legitimate flag bearer of the alliance; but this logic, was apparently not convincing to the NPP leader, Dr Azikiwe.

It should be noted that one of the features which encourages coalition, and consequently, multipartism in a parliamentary system, is the availability of two equally attractive and prestigious offices – Prime Minister and president. Perhaps compromise between Dr Azikiwe and Chief Awolowo could have been easily struck under such an arrangement. Dr Azikiwe's hint at a possible change to the parliamentary system[175] may not be unconnected with this feeling.

The failure to resolve the leadership deadlock was a major impediment to a merger; it appeared that the steps leading to a merger did not receive the enthusiastic support of the UPN leadership, much of which felt that such a

---

175. *West Africa*, 5 April 1982, p. 956.

merger should follow the 1983 election.[176] Chief Awolowo, with his eye on national leadership, might have feared that a merger could rob him of the opportunity to compete for the presidency due to a conspiracy by the other parties. Moreover, the sagacious Chief rationalised his unwillingness to step down for Dr Azikiwe on the age factor. Chief Awolowo was 74, while Dr Azikiwe was 78. The Chief was quoted to have said that, if he were ten years younger than Dr Azikiwe, he would probably have stepped down.[177] There was, however, no ambiguity as to the unifying effect of the presidency; Chief Awolowo indicated that the trend of the elections would dictate whom all members in the P.P.A. would support in the presidential election.[178]

However, the optimism that the "progressives" would co-operate in the course of the 1983 elections was done a fatal blow with a re-arrangement of their order. Unlike in 1979, the presidential election was the first to take place on the 6th of August. The election was won by the NPN candidate Alhaji Shehu Shagari, who polled 47.5% of the votes, while his rivals, Chief Obafemi Awolowo (UPN) and Dr Nnamdi Azikiwe (NPP) polled 31.2% and 14% respectively. The 1983 elections were greeted with violent protests in some states of the federation, because of allegations of electoral malpractices in gubernatorial and parliamentary elections, thus encouraging the military to again sack the democratic experiment on 31 December, 1983.

---

176. Alan Cowell, "In Nigerian Vote, Old Leaders Come Out Fighting," *New York Times,* 3 May 1982, p. 2.
177. *West Africa,* 3 January 1983, p. 22.
178. Ibid., p. 22.

CHAPTER SIX

FROM MANUFACTURING A TWO-PARTY SYSTEM TO A POTENTIAL TWO-PARTY SYSTEM

Following the sacking of the civilian politicians, General Muhammadu Buhari established a military administration. He immediately detained a category of prominent politicians and political office-holders who were assumed either to have enriched themselves unjustly or to have been responsible for the misdeeds of the previous era.[179] The administration's seeming hostility to debates about the restoration of democracy – a hostility encouraged by the unrestrained euphoria that had welcomed it into office – came from a misunderstanding of the nature of the Nigerian people. The administration soon antagonised the political class and the aspiring politicians. Its promulgation

---

179. For the causes of the failure of the second republic, see Toyin Falola, and Julius Inhonvbere, *The Rise and Fall of Nigeria's Second Republic, 1979-84* (London: 1985). See also Ladipo Adamolekun, *The Fall of the Second Republic* (Ibadan: 1985).

of Decree No.4 (Public Officer Protection Against False Accusation Decree) not only succeeded in emasculating the press, but also resulted in the imprisonment of some of its members. This meant that the administration soon lost the support and co-operation of an ally and influential constituency whose aggressive journalistic attacks on the corrupt politicians had served, more or less, as a barometer for the timing of the coup that brought the Buhari regime into power. General Buhari's iron-fisted approach to political governance had generated such a heated atmosphere that a palace coup by General Ibrahim Babangida, on 27 August 1985, although received with scepticism, was what was needed to restore confidence among an disenchanted citizenry.

General Babangida announced his arrival by revoking the troublesome Decree No.4, and declaring his intention to respect human rights. His administration sponsored public debates on important national issues, and by 13 January 1986, had inaugurated a 17-member Political Bureau, headed by Professor Sylvanus Cookey, whose terms of reference included, "The review of Nigeria's political history, identifying the basic problems which had led to failure in the past and suggesting ways of resolving and coping with those problems."[180] President Babangida enjoined the bureau to come up with a political arrangement that would be unique to Nigeria:

> *The administration does not want a regurgitation of the political models of the so-called advanced countries of the world. If this were our desire, we*

---

180. *West Africa* (London), 20 January 1986, p. 152.

would not have wasted your time, and ours, by inviting you here. Rather, we would simply have turned to the volumes and various encyclopaedias on these alien constitutions.[181]

The call on Nigerians to participate effectively in the debates resulted in vigorous discussions, particularly on the nature of the party system. Those who had viewed the institution of political parties to be responsible for the misfortune of Nigerian society called for its ejection from the political order. The typical 'anti-party' sentiment is this expressed by Itodo Ojobo:

It was the introduction of party politics by colonial administration that set off the fire of ethnic conflicts in Nigeria [...] it is party politics that causes discrimination, victimisation of political opponents. Parties train, arm and finance thugs to eliminate, harass and intimidate both political opponents and ordinary citizens alike. Rather than act as vehicles for social mobilisation, political, education, cohesion, integration and good government, parties in Nigeria have been instruments of coercion, exploitation and oppression of the innocent citizens of Nigeria.[182]

In what became popularly known as the 'Zero-Party Option', advocates asked the nation to adopt a "no-party system in which elections are based on personal or individual merit."[183] Other proponents of 'politics without parties' called for "representation through professional

---
181. Ibid., p. 152.
182. Cited by Jibrin Ibrahim in 'the Political Debate and the Struggle for Democracy in Nigeria', *Review of African Political Economy*, No. 37, December 1986, p. 45.
183. Federal Republic of Nigeria, *Report of the Political Bureau* (Lagos: 1987), p. 42.

associations, religious, cultural or productive groups."[184]

The Political Bureau was hardly impressed by the strongly-worded indictments arraigned against political parties, as it upheld the parties' inevitable role as "agents of political participation and mobilisation...[And] more importantly, a vehicle for the aggregation of demands and also an agent of national integration."[185]

Consequently, the bureau was left with a choice between a one-party system and a multi-party system, which, according to their report, were the other options proposed by Nigerians. Asserting that the basic argument in favour of the latter was the freedom of association of groups and individuals in a truly democratic society, the body hinted that the number of parties recommended in the debate ranged from two to five, of which its preference "was for a two-party system, with only one member dissenting in favour of a one-party system".[186]

The decision of the Political Bureau to limit party competition to two, apart from the apparent definitional confusion of a two-party with a multi-party system, has indeed been highly controversial. The bureau justified its recommendation in the belief that the two-party arrangement would lead to Nigeria's politics being based on principles and not ethnicity. The argument was made that since past political groupings had tended to revolve around the country's three major ethnic divisions (Hausa-Fulani in the North, Ibo in the South-East, and Yoruba in the South-West) such an arrangement would force groups to work together. This, however, is contradicted by the

---

184. Ibid., p. 42.
185. *Report of the Political Bureau*, p. 42.
186. Ibid., p. 42

bureau's observation that "although at the beginning of each political era, many parties were registered in Nigeria, sooner or later, the system gravitated towards a two-party system."[187]

The government accepted the recommendation as part of the programme for a return to civilian rule, scheduled for 1992, and entrenched the two-party system in the Nigerian Constitution. The idea of a two-party system tallied with President Babangida's thinking; he had revealed earlier, in an interview, that he did not think more than three political parties should be allowed to compete. And Mr Ovie-Whiskey, chairman of the disbanded Federal Electoral Commission, had suggested that the work of the commission would be made less cumbersome by limiting the number of political parties to two.

However, according to the Political Bureau, the following strict conditions had first to be met:

(a) That both political parties accept the national philosophy of government;

(b) That the differences between the political parties concern the priorities and strategies of implementation of the national objectives;

(c) That their membership be open to every citizen of Nigeria irrespective of place of origin, sex, religion, or ethnic grouping;

(d) That the national executive organ and the

---

187. Ibid., p. 42

principal officers of each political party reflect the Federal character of Nigeria.[188]

In strict adherence to the outlined programme of return to civilian rule, General Babangida lifted the ban on party politics in May 1989. Meanwhile, he had imposed an almost blanket ban on a category of ex-politicians and previous office-holders from running for office. In a broadcast to the nation, the President had, in June 1987, announced that, "All past politicians are banned from seeking or holding any public office for a period of ten years, effective from the date of lifting of the ban on politics".[189] This was again modified in September 1987; the ban, which now included him, would be lifted after the 1992 presidential elections.[190] Those who have been found guilty of corruption and other misdeeds were to be banned forever. General Babangida emphasised that, "The decision should be seen not as a punitive measure, but as a necessary step to give Nigeria a fair chance to develop a new culture and leadership."[191]

Creating Two New Political Parties

Following the lifting of the ban, about 35 political associations canvassed for support, or got their names mentioned in the newspapers, but in the end, only thirteen of them felt prepared to apply to the National Electoral Commission for a place among the two parties to be

---

188. Ibid., p. 42-43.
189. "Former Political Office Holders and a New Political Morality", *West Africa,* 31 August 1987, p. 1690.
190. "Towards a new political order?", *West Africa,* 5 October 1987, p. 1951.
191. *National Concord,* 03 September 1987.

registered. The thirteen political associations were:

(1) All Nigeria People's Party (ANPP);
(2) Ideal People's Party (IPP);
(3) Liberal Convention (LC);
(4) Nigeria Labour Party (NLP);
(5) Nigerian National Congress (NNC);
(6) Nigeria People's Welfare Party (NPWP);
(7) National Union Party (NUP);
(8) People's Front of Nigeria (PFN);
(9) Patriotic Nigerian Party (PNP)
(10) Patriotic People's Party (PPP);
(11) People's Solidarity Party (PSP);
(12) Republican Party (RP);
(13) United Nigeria Democratic Party (UNDP).

The commission had come up with the following guidelines:

(1) Each political association shall state the number of its registered members, age and residential address of each member to facilitate physical confirmation;

(2) A non-refundable registration fee of ₦50,000 (fifty thousand Naira) shall be sent to the NEC;

(3) Each association to submit to the NEC a statement of its assets and liabilities at the time it is applying for registration;

(4) No person affected by the Participation in Politics and Elections (Prohibition) Decree 9 of 1989 shall be eligible for holding an executive position in a political association;[192]

(5) All members of the national executive committee of the political association shall each, individually, submit statements of their assets and liabilities, sworn to in an affidavit in High Court, with the association's application for registration;

(6) No alien shall be eligible to hold office in, or to be a founding, ordinary or other member of, a political association.[193]

The NEC also required associations seeking registration to indicate in their manifesto how they intended to tackle the country's political and socio-economic problems. Except for a few associations whose members probably sought to impress the NEC with their preparedness for registration, most of the political associations considered the requirements to be rather cumbersome. This tended to compel talks about mergers between one group and another – something which President Babangida had asked the groups to do. However, observing the short duration between the lifting of the ban on politics in May and the close of applications for registration in July, Professor Wole Soyinka commented rather cynically that "any party which

---

192. Contravention of this decree carries a fine of N250,000 (two hundred and fifty thousand naira), or an imprisonment for a period of five years, or both. Alhaji Balarabe Musa, the impeached Governor of Kaduna State, was charged with contravening the decree.
193. *West Africa*, 15 May 1989.

fulfils the conditions of the NEC should be automatically disqualified because it can only mean that they've been organising before the ban was lifted."[194] The outspoken leader of the Nigerian People's Welfare Party, Chief G.B.A. Akinyede, also considered it "unrealistic for NEC to expect political associations to register an average of one million supporters who are required to provide passport photographs at a total cost of N10 million, and still proclaim that members of such parties are the common people of Nigeria".[195] On another occasion, he insisted that "only political criminals can satisfy NEC's requirements going by the cost of what they demanded."[196] To fulfil these requirements in only two months, he added, "one would have either emptied the treasury through inflated contracts in Abuja (the nation's new capital) or elsewhere, lifted petroleum illegally or pushed cocaine."[197]

Similarly, legitimate questions were asked as to what would happen were more than two groups to fulfil the requirements.[198] Such questions, however, were academic, as the Armed Forces Ruling Council (AFRC) had vested in itself the power and authority to decide the two political associations that were qualified. There was also the view that registering only two out of thirteen political associations could amount to registering the minority

---

194. Quoted in *Nigeria Focus* (London), 31 August 1989.
195. *National Concord* (Lagos), 19 June 1989.
196. Ibid., 21 September 1989.
197. Ibid., 21 September 1989.
198. See, for instance, Anthony A. Akinola, 'Parties and Precedents', *West Africa,* 27 July 1987, pp. 1441, 1442; Larry Diamond in *Democracy in Developing Countries Vol. 2: Africa,* (Boulder, CO, 1988), and Ojukwu on Party Registration, *National Concord* (Lagos), 27 July 1989, p. 9.

against the majority of the Nigerian population.[199] To ensure fairness, the suggestion was made that all the political associations should be allowed to contest in the local government elections scheduled for December 1989, following which the two most successful of them would be registered as political parties. This suggestion, in itself, had merit; the absurdity and crudeness in it was to be found in the necessity of asking a mass of people and their elected councillors to switch support to political parties they had already rejected at the polls.[200] Its potential for causing civil disorder was enormous; the political associations would have been likely to engage in a bitter contest, with disputes over the outcome of elections resulting in violence. So, perhaps fortunately, both the NEC and the AFRC seemed not to pay attention to this suggestion, sticking by the approach that they had already chosen. Nevertheless, President Babangida did not spare any available opportunity to convince the Nigerian populace of the impartiality of his administration over the registration exercise and gain their trust and confidence. In a broadcast to the nation on 27 August 1989, he emphasised that:

> *The registration of two political parties will be another important milestone in [Nigeria's] journey to a democratic polity [...] This administration has no vested interest in the registration of any particular*

---

199. See Wale Oshodi, 'Dilemma of Political Associations', in *National Concord*, 16 September 1989.
200. *Newswatch* (Lagos), 25 September 1989, 24. For instance, Ezekiel Izuogu, PSP's national secretary, is quoted as saying that 'all the political associations should contest the December local government elections if we truly believe in democracy in the Third Republic'.

> *political association as a political party. The criteria for registration of political parties have already been spelt out by the NEC. I wish to assure the nation that [the] political associations will be assessed on these criteria, and no extraneous considerations will be allowed to influence the outcome of the party registration exercise.*[201]

However, appreciating the significance of the military in the process of registering the political parties, the various political associations did their best to impress the government by promising to uphold its economic programmes. Mindful of the fact that many Nigerians had expressed dissatisfaction with the regime's IMF-directed Structural Adjustment Programme (SAP), some of the associations promised to give it a 'human face'. For instance, Dr. Okupe, deputy publicity secretary of the Liberal Convention, promised that his association would "carry out some adjustments in the economic programme", emphasising that "with the present and financial policies of the Federal Government and some necessary adjustment, it is certain that the ultimate goal of economic emancipation will be attained in due course."[202] They also warned that the banned politicians were not accommodated in their groups, as this extract from an advert reveals:

> *[Our association] is not floated by the top brass of yesterday, or by the gang of airline magnates, shipping barons or petroleum lifters. It is not a party of past governors or ministers, election riggers,*

---

201. 'Posterity will justify our Actions', *Nigerian Tribune* (Ibadan), 28 August 1989.
202. 'LC will Continue SAP', *National Concord,* 12 September 1989.

counterfeit makers or import licence racketeers or rice importers. But on the other hand it does not comprise of the communists or the socialists. [203]

The NEC submitted its report to the AFRC in September, having verified the claims made by the political associations – verification which included an examination of documents which some of the associations had conveyed to the NEC secretariat with much fanfare, in various types of vehicles.[204] In the report, the electoral commission had observed, among other shortcomings, that:

(1) The associations 'made exaggerated claims about their membership size and organisational strength'. They reflected a total membership size of only 467,132 out of a projected registrable [adult] population of 60.3 million Nigerians.[205] The associations claimed to have registered 1,635,485 members, which means that 'out of every 10 claims made by the associations more that 7 could not be verified';

---

203. 'Nigeria People's Welfare Party', *National Concord*, 7 July 1989, 14. General Babangida's apparent dislike for the radicals whom he had described as 'extremists' who must not participate in the political process, is responsible for the advertisers' emphasis on the party not harbouring 'communists and socialists'.

204. One political association, for instance, conveyed its documents in 22 lorries, one representing the National Capital Territory and the remaining 21 representing each of the 21 states of the Federation.

205. The poor membership registration in each of the political associations can be attributed to a growing apathy about party politics – apathy which is deeply rooted in unpalatable experiences with past political activities; for example, the excruciating state of the nation's economy and its impact on the individual, together with the NEC's requirement of passport photographs from people who could least afford such a 'luxury'. And, of course, the insufficiency of time for the associations to canvass for support.

(2) Virtually all the associations were rent by factionalism as a result of power struggles which portend ill for the Third Republic;

(3) Most of the associations were traceable to the banned political parties of the past 'whose burden must be shed if the country is to move forward';

(4) The NEC was unable to determine, owing to lack of vital information, the extent of foreign financing and external backing "which would have gone a long way in helping [the body] to make a firm determination of the registrability or otherwise of the associations."[206]

Consequently, the NEC could not give its stamp of authority to any two of the political associations as none had fulfilled the requirements. However, the Commission drew up a shortlist of six associations in order of priority in which [they] have best satisfied the condition, expecting the government to select two. Out of a possible score of 100 [50 for membership spread and size, 30 for administrative organisation and 20 for manifestos and essays], the People's Solidarity Party came first with 43.90, followed by Nigerian National Congress (42.62), the People's Front of Nigeria (41.20) and the Liberal Convention (34.08). The Nigerian Labour Party and the Republican Party of

---

206. See *National Concord*, 28 September 1989, for the NEC's report. See also, in the same paper, the useful analysis of Tunji Bello, political editor.

Nigeria were placed fifth and sixth with 17.90 and 17.00 respectively.[207]

The three leading associations, PSP, NNC, and PFN, were believed to be affiliated to the banned political parties of the Second Republic. The PSP was viewed as the reincarnation of the Progressive Parties Alliance (PPA) which comprised of the Unity Party of Nigeria (UPN), Nigerian People's Party (NPP), Great Nigerian People's Party (GNPP), and a faction of the People's Redemption Party (PRP). The NNC was perceived as the protrusion of the former ruling party, the National Party of Nigeria (NPN), while the PFN was "seen as a splinter group of the NPN, now trying to go it alone."[208] The leadership of the fourth-ranked Liberal Convention wanted to cash in on these perceptions by singing its own praises; "Everyone knows that all the others are re-incarnations of old political groupings. The LC should, therefore, be given credit for emanating from nothing, without any existing structures to be among the big four. We hope the government will continue in its consistency and register only truly new breed groups."[209]

While they were anxiously awaiting the verdict of the AFRC, reactions to the NEC's recommendations varied from one political association to the other. The PSP directorate described the NEC report "as the opinion of the people,"[210] while the NNC, in a one-page statement entitled 'People have spoken,' instructed its state and local government

---

207. Ibid.
208. *Newswatch*, 25 September 1989.
209. Ibid; quote belongs to Chief Onwuka Kalu, a prominent leader of the Liberal Convention.
210. *Weekend Concord* (Lagos), 30 September 1989.

directorate not to issue any press statement on the findings.²¹¹ This cautious optimism from both the PSP and NNC contrasted sharply with the seeming disappointment of the PFN and the LC. The former described the NEC report as "a non-committal and inconclusive technical document, that should be declared null and void,"²¹² while the latter called on the government to compel the six recommended political associations to a public debate that would inform Nigerians "about the associations' programmes, and how they intend to take the nation out of (its) current economic doldrums."²¹³ The Nigeria People's Welfare Party, which came last among the thirteen political associations, did not fail to express its disappointment; it filed an injunction at a Lagos High Court asking the AFRC "to completely disregard and discountenance the report in so far as it relates to guiding them in their duty of selecting, approving and recognising the two political parties."²¹⁴

The AFRC met on 5th October to discuss the NEC report. On 7th October, in a nationwide broadcast²¹⁵, Babangida told Nigerians of the dissolution of the thirteen political associations on the grounds that they were rooted in ethnic and religious bigotry and, therefore, did not meet "our vision of a new political order."²¹⁶ Consequently, he announced the creation of two new political parties, the Social Democratic Party (SDP) and the National Republican Convention (NRC), which Nigerians were to choose

---

211. 'NNC Gives Shut-up Order', *National Concord*, 29 September 1989.
212. *Weekend Concord*, 30 September 1989.
213. Ibid., 30 September 1989.
214. 'AFRC, NEC Dragged to Court', *National Concord*, 5 October 1989.
215. *National Concord*, 8 October 1989, page unknown.
216. Ibid., 8 October 1989.

between on an individual basis. The two political parties, "one a little to the left of centre and the other a little to the right of centre", would be organised and financed by the military under a new "grassroots democratic two-party system."[217] The ₦50,000 deposits paid to the NEC by each of the political associations were refunded to them, while the political parties were provided with identical offices in the Federal Capital and at each of the state and local government headquarters.

Between Optimism and Pessimism

General Babangida's creation of the two political parties was considered by many commentators as artificial, if not bizarre. According to Olu Onagoruwa, a Nigerian constitutional lawyer, "The normal practice in the history of constitutional government is for people to create parties and parties then to create government. But Babangida has reversed historical experience and common sense by making government to create parties and parties to create people."[218] Professor Wole Soyinka, who spoke approvingly of the creation of the two political parties, disagreed with the imposition of manifestos by the government, saying that, "A voodoo type democracy product was weird enough, but the imposition of manifestoes was carrying the principle of unity of opposites to new mystical heights."[219]

---

217. Ibid., 8 October 1989.
218. *Newswatch,* 13 November 1989.
219. *West Africa,* 12-18 March 1990, p. 427. The manifestos of the two political parties can hardly be distinguished from one another: 'some sceptics have already decided that the two barely distinguishable platforms will take second place to more fundamental ethnic and religious issues'. See Michael Holman, *Financial Times* (London), 19 March 1990.

Nevertheless, General Babangida's formula was greeted with loud acclaim by a large segment of the Nigerian population, who blamed the politicians for lack of discipline and organisation.[220] Professor Humphery Nwosu, the NEC chairman, believed that the creation of the two parties would give:

> *Equal rights and opportunities to all Nigerians to participate in the political process, irrespective of their wealth, religious background and status, de-emphasise the role of money in politics, reduce violence in electoral process, ensure the emergence of new leadership that will not be proxy for old political warlords, and give Nigerians a new political structure within which to operate - avoiding political alliances along the same lines as the first and second parties, among other things.*[221]

Professor Nwosu more or less echoed the view of the prominent proponents of the two-party system; Dr Chuba Okadigbo, former Political Adviser to ex-President Shehu Shagari, and Professor Sam Egite Oyovbaire, a respected Nigerian academic who had served as a member of the Political Bureau. Okadigo argued that, with Babangida calling for the imposition of the two-party system by constitutional or administrative fiat:

---

220. Both the *Sunday Concord* (Lagos) and *Newswatch* declared President Babangida their 'Man of the Year' for 1989 as a result of his artificial creation of parties.
221. *West Africa*, 23-29 October 1989, p. 1777.

when one party is in government, the other will function as the credible alternative. Where a party in power is aware of its potentials for loss at the next election, and also knows that the other party has a credible national base, the incumbent party is more than likely to think and work harder and to force its leadership to adopt humane and political procedures [...] it is the availability of a third party or more parties, as nuisance rather than as credible alternative that engenders confusion.[222]

Okadigbo's 'Lowelian' advocacy of a two-party system of "two and two parties only" had a supporter in Sam Oyovbaire.[223] The latter viewed the two-party system strictly from an ideological point of view, believing that it would "set the stage for the gradual clarification of our choice or locus in accordance with the two great historical systems of capitalism and socialism."[224] Although the Political Bureau recommended that the political parties accept the national philosophy of government, something which could hardly be pre-determined on paper, Professor Oyovbaire's enthusiasm for ideological polarisation is nevertheless an important idea to be examined.

---

222. Chuba Okadigbo, 'Creating the New Out of the Old', in *African Concord* (London), 20 February 1986, 17-18; see also, *Power and Leadership in Nigeria* (Enugu, 1987). For a view that a two-party system cannot be decreed into existence, see B.J. Dudley, *Instability and Political Order; Politics and Crisis in Nigeria* (Ibadan: 1973), p. 251.

223. Lawrence Lowell suggested that the legislature must contain only two political parties, 'in order that the parliamentary form of government should permanently produce good results'. See *Government and Parties in Continental Europe* (Boston: 1986).

224. Sam Egite Oyovbaire, 'Can the Civilians Triumph?', *African Concord,* 12 February 1988.

The two-party proposal had a host of other adherents. Dr. Tunde Adeniran, who was also a member of the Political Bureau, helpfully assembled the arguments upon which they rested their case:[225]

(1) That the tasks before Nigerians in the next few decades are urgent and extremely difficult and would therefore require some degree of regimentation. Short of a one-party state which the majority of Nigerians opposed during the political debate, the two-party option is the best alternative;

(2) That a two-party system provides the electorate with opportunities of choice and thus enables the masses to determine who governs them and how they are governed.

(3) That it allows for opposition. The duty of the opposition is to criticise the lapses of the government, and, in this way, get the government to strive towards excellence in the task of governance;

(4) That the people's power of determining who rules them (under a two-party system) and the regular and smooth elections constitute the strong point of inter-party competition under the two-party system;

(5) That a two-party system is best for Nigeria's heterogeneous society. This is because [unlike in the past when ethnic, tribal and religious

---

225. Dr Tunde Adeniran, 'The Two-Party System and the Federal Political Process' (unpublished manuscript), p. 11.

sentiments dominated the political scene] issues – not persons and parochialism – will predominate [in the] electoral process.

The Premature Death of an 'experiment'

The two government-sponsored political parties, with identical party offices in each of the then thirty states of the Federation as well as the federal capital of Abuja, took off on a rather optimistic note. They were mainly embraced by 'new breed' politicians and supporters who seemed determined to make a success of the new experiment in political engineering. In the 1991 governorship elections, the Social Democratic Party (SDP) won in fourteen states, while the rival National Republican Convention (NRC) won in sixteen.[226] Nigerians were seemingly getting used to identifying themselves as 'Democrats' and 'Republicans', just like the American voters whose political order the authors of Nigeria's manufactured two-party system wanted to ape.

However, the acid test of Babangida's 'gimmickry' came in the presidential election of June 12, 1993. It proved to be a test of honesty on the part of the general, who had postponed transitional elections on two previous occasions, 1990 and 1992. The 1993 election would have led to a transfer of political power from General Babangida to a democratically-elected president of the federal republic.

The 1993 presidential election was keenly contested by the two well-balanced political parties; Chief Moshood Abiola was the candidate of the SDP, while Alhaji Bashir

---

226. Presidential Elections in Nigeria, *African Elections Database* (1999, 2003, 2007, and 2011, respectively).

Tofa was that of the NRC. The election, judged to have been relatively free and fair, was widely believed to have been won by Moshood Abiola, a well-known business mogul and philanthropist. His rival had been relatively unknown.

However, General Ibrahim Babangida, apparently still wanting to hang onto power, annulled the election won by his "personal friend", thereby provoking a crisis which forced him to "step aside" on 27 August, 1993.[227] Chief Abiola was a Yoruba Muslim from the South, while Alhaji Tofa was a Hausa Muslim from the North.

The Babangida administration was succeeded by a hastily cobbled-together Interim National Government (ING), led by Chief Ernest Shonekan, a successful industrialist who hailed from Abiola's hometown of Abeokuta. However, the 'ING contraption' was quickly brushed aside on November 17, 1993, by General Sani Abacha, erstwhile second-in-command to General Babangida.

General Abacha seemed determined to fully establish his own rule and this meant Chief Moshood Abiola's anxiety to claim the mandate he had been denied by Babangida was one nuisance Abacha would not tolerate. He kept Abiola in detention; however, both Abacha and Abiola died in mysterious circumstances on 8 June and 7 July, 1998 respectively.

---

227. See, for instance, Max Siollun, "What if Abiola had Become President?", *maxsiollun.wordpress.com*, June 2, 2008. See also, Anthony Akinola, "The Legacy of June 12", *Daily Trust*, June 13, 2011.

Towards a New Order

The annulment of the 1993 presidential election, which Nigerians now simply refer to as 'June 12', was most vehemently resented in the South, not least because the North had dominated the leadership position since the country's independence in 1960. It was in the light of the ensuing crisis that a new military ruler, General Abdusalami Abubakar, hurriedly organised a transitional election, at which the presidency was conceded to the South, the regional base of the defrauded Chief Moshood Abiola.

Meanwhile, the politicians had formed new political parties – the People's Democratic Party (PDP), Alliance for Democracy (AD) and the All Peoples Party (APP) which were described as "old wine in new bottles".[228] The rather conservative PDP adopted General Olusegun Obasanjo, erstwhile military ruler from February 1976 to October 1979, as its presidential candidate, while the relatively more progressive and liberal AD/APP alliance presented Chief Olu Falae, erstwhile Finance Minister in the regime of General Ibrahim Babangida, as their flag-bearer. Both Obasanjo and Falae were Yoruba and Christian from the South-West geo-political zone. General Olusegun Obasanjo prevailed in the 1999 presidential election; the table's below provide a quick glance at the dominance of the People's Democratic Party (PDP) in the presidential elections of 1999, 2003, 2007 and 2011 respectively.[229]

---

228. The PDP drew its strength from the North and has correlations with the defunct National Party of Nigeria (NPN), while the AD was confined to the South-West region populated by the Yoruba. The APP was popular in Kano, the stronghold of the defunct Aminu Kano's radical NEPU and later, the PRP.
229. Except for the 1999 presidential election contested between two candidates, subsequent elections featured quite a number of contestants not listed here.

The 1999 Presidential Election

Candidates	Party	Votes	%
Olusegun Obasanjo	People's Democratic Party	18,738,154	62.78
Olu Falae	Alliance for Democracy (AD) – All Peoples Party (APP)	11,110,287	37.22

The 2003 Presidential Election

Candidates	Party	Votes	%
Olusegun Obasanjo	People's Democratic Party	24,456,140	61.94
Muhammadu Buhari	All Nigeria Peoples Party (ANPP)	12,710,022	32.19
Odumegwu Ojukwu	All Progressives Grand Alliance	1,297,445	3.29

The 2007 Presidential Election

Candidates	Party	Votes	%
Umaru Yar'Adua	People's Democratic Party (PDP)	24,638,063	69.82
Muhammadu Buhari	All Nigeria Peoples Party (ANPP)	6,605,299	18.72
Atiku Abubakar	Action Congress (AC)	2,637,848	7.47

The 2011 Presidential Election

Candidates	Party	Votes	%
Goodluck Jonathan	People's Democratic Party (PDP)	22,495,187	58.89
Muhammadu Buhari	Congress for Progressive Change (CPC)	12,214,853	31.98
Nuhu Ribadu	Action Congress of Nigeria (ACN)	2,079,159	5.41
Ibrahim Shekarau	All Nigeria Peoples Party (ANPP)	917,012	2.40

The dominance of the PDP, even when over-exaggerated in a culture of fraudulent elections, was sufficient cause of concern for any other political party whose leader had genuine aspirations for the presidency. Furthermore, the PDP was the only political party whose support base traversed the various divides.

General Muhammadu Buhari of the Congress for Progressive Change had unsuccessfully competed for the presidency on two previous occasions, 2003 and 2007. It was clear that he needed support from the South in anticipation of the 2011 presidential elections. The CPC, which he had hastily cobbled together in 2010, revolved around him as a figurehead and was limited to the North.

As such, Buhari sought an alliance with the Action Congress of Nigeria (ACN),[230] led by Senator Ahmed Bola

---

230. Alhaji Atiku Abubakar contested the 2007 presidential election on the platform of Action Congress, having disagreed with his boss, General Olusegun Obasanjo, over the latter's perceived extra-constitutional 'third-term' agenda. The AC was a re-incarnation of the AD, a party that boasted of loyalists to Chief Obafemi Awolowo, the founder of the Action Group and the Unity Party of Nigeria.

Tinubu. The ACN had a formidable followership in the South-West, populated by the Yoruba. The quest for an alliance did not, in the end, bear fruit for the 2011 elections; however, it provided the platform for what would be a significant future development.

The opportunities for political alliance widened, now actively promoted by governors elected on the platforms of ACN, CPC, ANPP, and a faction of the All Progressive Grand Alliance (APGA). These political parties, identified by their claims of progressive ideology, formed the All Progressives Congress (APC) political party, as seen in the table above, in February 2013. The party was formally registered by the Independent National Electoral Commission (INEC) on 31 July 2013 – a significant development in the history of political party formation in Nigeria.

PROSPECTS AND CHALLENGES FOR THE FUTURE

The emergence of the unified progressive party, the All Progressives Congress (APC), more or less coincided with the emergence of an internal crisis in the ruling People's Democratic Party (PDP).

The main causes of the crisis can be briefly summarised as the following: 1. A frosty relationship between President Goodluck Jonathan and Governor Rotimi Amaechi of Rivers State[231]; 2. An allegation of arbitrariness on the part of the immediate past PDP Chairman, Alhaji Bamanga Tukur[232]; and 3. The perceived ambition of President

---

231. Eddy Odivwri, "Recasting the Jonathan-Amaechi Rift", *This Day,* 18 May 2013.
232. Zayyad Muhammad, "Between BamangaTukur and Gov Murtala Nyako", *Pointblanknews.com,* undated.

Jonathan to seek re-election in 2015 in contradiction of a supposed agreement that he would not be doing so.[233]

The aggrieved parties found a common ground, forcefully expressing their disagreements with the PDP leadership. When Governor Rotimi Amaechi sought re-election as Chairman of the Nigerian Governors' Forum (NGF) on 24 May, 2013, the party leadership opposed his bid and opted for Governor Jonah Jang, PDP governor of Plateau State.[234] However, Mr Amaechi won the election, scoring 19 votes to Jang's 16.[235] The PDP leadership refused to recognise the outcome of that election.[236]

Governor Amaechi's re-election was actively supported by those governors whose parties would later be officially registered as the APC on 31 July, 2013. They gave their support to allow them exploit disagreements in the PDP to their own political advantage. Governor Amaechi was also actively supported by the co-aggrieved PDP governors. The latter, including Amaechi, would later be identified as G7 Governors.[237]

The G7 governors – Sule Lamido (Jigawa), Abdulfatah Ahmed (Kwara), Aliyu Wamakko (Sokoto), Musa Kwankwaso (Kano), Rotimi Amaechi (Rivers), Murtala

---

233. "Babangida Aliyu: Jonathan Agreed to Serve One Term", *This Day,* 17 February 2013. See also Obasanjo's "Before It Is Too Late – an Open Letter to Goodluck Jonathan", *Daily Trust,* 23 December 2013.
234. Olalekan Adetayo, "Amaechi not NGF chairman, Presidency insists", *The Punch,* 18 November 2013.
235. There are 36 state governors; Governor Ibrahim Gaidam of Yobe State was absent.
236. "Amaechi not NGF chairman, Presidency insists", *The Punch,* 18 November 2013.
237. Kunle Oderemi and Olawale Rasheed, "News Analysis: Genesis of PDP Crisis and Implications of defections", *The Tribune,* 27 November 2013.

Nyako (Adamawa) and Babangida Aliyu (Niger) – crisscrossed the nation, sharing their grievances with former national leaders, who included Olusegun Obasanjo, Ibrahim Babangida, and Abdulsalam Abubakar.[238] They also held meetings with President Goodluck Jonathan.[239]

On 31 August, 2013, the PDP held a special national convention. The names of candidates for election excluded those of supporters of the aggrieved governors.[240] Infuriated, the governors walked out of the convention hall and immediately announced the emergence of a new political party, the "New PDP".[241] The leadership of the new party included erstwhile Vice President Atiku Abubakar. The Chairman of the New PDP, Abubakar Kawu Baraje, "identified violations of the PDP constitution committed by the Tukur leadership to include the change of the date for the special convention from 20 July to 31 August without reverting to the National Executive Committee of the party."[242]

On 26 November, 2013, five of the aggrieved governors "formally" defected to the rival APC, in what was celebrated as an "APC/New PDP merger".[243] The five governors were: Aliyu Wamakko, Rotimi Amaechi, Murtala Nyako, Abdulfatah Ahmed, and Musa Kwankwaso. The spate of

---

238. See, for instance, "Obasanjo, G7 Governors Meet in Abeokuta", *This Day*, 5 Nov 2013.
239. Ben Agande, "Jonathan returns, to meet G7 governors this week", *The Vanguard*, 24 November 2013.
240. "Convention shocker: PDP Splits!", *The Vanguard*, 1 September 2013.
241. Ibid., 1 September 2013.
242. "PDP Splits as Atiku, Seven Governors Form "NewPDP", *This Day*, 1 September 2013.
243. Festus Owete, "APC merges with New PDP", *Premium Times*, 26 November 2013.

defections consequently intruded into the House of Representatives, where 37 PDP law-makers joined the All Progressives Congress. "The development increased the numerical strength of the APC from 135 to 172. With this, it has a simple majority in the House as the PDP now has 171 members."[244] Most of the defectors were from Kano, Rivers, Kwara and Sokoto.[245]

With quite a number of PDP politicians defecting to the APC, commentators wondered if the latter had compromised their ideological principles.[246] However, Alhaji Atiku Abubaakar described the development as good for democracy, saying, "It is good for democracy. I have always supported a two-party system."[247] For Dr Kayode Fayemi, APC Governor of Ekiti State, "the merger of the new People's Democratic Party (nPDP) with the All Progressives Congress (APC) is a signal that alternation of power at the federal level is imminent."[248]

With politicians perpetually seeking platforms from which to actualise their ambitions, the spate of defections will continue into the future. Apart from the big parties, PDP and APC, the Labour Party is one small party that seems to be doing reasonably well.[249] According to Bolaji

---

244. John Ameh and Olusola Fabiyi, "37 Reps defect to APC", *The Punch*, 19 December 2013.
245. Chido Onumah, "Is APC the New PDP", *Sahara Reporter*, 26 December 2013.
246. Ibid., 26 December 2013
247. Raphael Adeyanju, "Atiku: APC, New PDP Merger Good for Nigeria", *Daily Newswatch*, undated.
248. "APC, nPDP Merger: Alternation of Power Is Imminent – Fayemi", APC FAN CLUB – Worldwide, 27 November 2013.
249. There have been a few defections from the major parties to Labour. For instance, Michael Opeyemi Bamidele, a member of the House of Representatives, defected from the APC to Labour as he could not secure the former's endorsement for him to contest the Ekiti governorship election due in June.

Akinyemi, professor of political science and former External Affairs Minister, "The Labour Party in Nigeria will always be for those of us who want to vote with our conscience. The Labour Party may never win an election in the presidency but they will make you feel that you still voted but not for either of those two characters."[250]

For those who seek ideological purity, it requires stating here that any given political party is a product of its environment. In a society as heterogeneous as Nigeria, the broad-based political party would inevitably accommodate cultural, ethnic, and religious diversities as well as the temperaments they express. The United States of America is one heterogeneous society with the most visible two-party system in the world. However, the party system has been described as "at best loose alliances of highly disparate interests" and "like a four-party system consisting of liberal Democrats, conservative Democrats, liberal Republicans, and conservative Republicans", "a six-party system with left, centre and right wings in each party", or "even a hundred-party system with different Democratic and Republican parties in each of the 50 states."[251] This could be the scenario for the Nigerian party system.

In the present day, the People's Democratic Party (PDP) and the newly-registered All Progressives Congress (APC) present two strong parties while minor parties or third parties are still able to exist along with them. The stage is thus set for a prospective two-party competition. The existence of competitive, broad-based political parties

---

250. "Prof Bolaji, Akinyemi At 72: Boko Haram lesson for Nigeria: stop ignoring grievances", *The Vanguard*, 5 January 2014.
251. Arend Lijphart, *Democracies: Patterns of Majoritarian and Consensus Government in Twenty-One Countries* (New Haven and London, 1984), p. 115.

undoubtedly provides the voter with viable alternatives. However, three issues are critical to the sustenance of the envisaged competition.

First, Nigerian electoral management has been, historically, problematic. Past elections were marred by allegations of rigging, voter intimidation, and even violence. Apart from a history of shoddy logistical preparations, Nigeria's electoral officials have failed to live up to the expectations of independent and impartial judges. All these problems would have to change, as two-party competition is an acceptance, on both sides, of equal loyalty to the democratic order.

The second crucial issue has to do with leadership recruitment. The truth of the matter is that loyalty to one's ethnicity or religion is still more potent in Nigerian politics than loyalty to ideology. Hence the quest for leadership has been disruptive in such a severely divided nation. To counter this issue, the PDP has adopted a principle of alternating the presidency between the North and the South; however, the principle suffered a major setback when President Umaru Yar'Adua died in office in May 2010, prompting controversial arguments as to the eligibility of incumbent President Goodluck Jonathan, a southerner, to seek re-election in 2015.[252] The Nigerian constitutionalists would have to find a realistic solution to the leadership question if the nation is to survive. The principle of leadership rotation seems appropriate in the context of the ethnological realities of the Nigerian nation: "Ideally what happens in a true democracy is for a president to be elected

---

252. Anthony A. Akinola, *Democracy in Nigeria: Thoughts and Selected Commentaries* (Rossendale Books, 2013), pp. 79-85.

from anywhere based on his personal merit, no matter where he comes from. But Nigeria is not an ideal county, so where the president comes from is still a very potent factor in the government and peace of the country."[253]

Finally, the issue of corruption poses great danger to the future of democracy in the Nigerian society. It would be recalled by voters and politicians alike that the military intervened in elections on two occasions (January 1966 and December 1983), accusing the politicians, among other things, of corruption. Corruption is a frightening issue and it shows no sign of abating. There is also the related issue of greed-elected politicians, who award outrageous salaries and allowances to themselves, leaving very little for development. Most now go into politics to accumulate wealth, hence the do or die attitude in electoral contests. The collective will of Nigerians would have to tame the monsters of corruption and greed.

---

253. Chief Mbazulike Amaehi in "2015 Presidency: North Should Wait for Now", *The Guardian* (Nigeria) 9 August 2013, p. 1.

BIBLIOGRAPHY

BOOKS

Adamolekun, Ladipo, *The Fall of the Second Republic* (Ibadan, 1985).

Ademoyega, Adewale, *Why We Struck* (Evans Brothers Nigeria Publishers-Limited, 1981).

Akinola, Anthony A., *Democracy in Nigeria: Thoughts and Selected Commentaries* (Rossendale Books, 2013).

Akintoye, S.A., *Emergent African States: Topics in Twentieth Century African History* (London: Longman Group Ltd., 1976).

Almond, Gabriel and Coleman, James, *The Politics of the Developing Areas* (New Jersey: Princeton University Press, 1964).

Arikpo, Okoi, *Development of Modern Nigeria* (Baltimore: Penguin Books, 1967).

Awa, Eme O., *Federal Government in Nigeria* (Berkeley and Los Angeles: University of California Press, 1964).

Awolowo, Obafemi, *Awo: The Autobiography of Chief Obafemi Awolowo* (Cambridge: University Press, 1960), p. 214.

Awolowo, Obafemi, *Awo on the Nigerian Civil War* (Ikeja, Nigeria: John West Publications Ltd., 1981).

Awolowo, Obafemi, *The People's Republic* (Ibadan: Oxford University Press, 1968).

Azikiwe, Nnamdi, *Selected Speeches of Dr. Nnamdi Azikiwe* (London: Cambridge University Press, 1961).

Azikiwe, Nnamdi, *The Development of Political Parties in Nigeria* (London: Office of the Commissioner in the United Kingdom for the Eastern Region of Nigeria, 1957).

Buell, Raymond Leslie, *The Native Problem in Africa* (New York: The MacMillan Company, 1928).

Coleman, James S., *Nigeria: Background to Nationalism* (Berkeley and Los Angeles: University of California Press, 1958).

Diamond, Larry, in *Democracy in Developing Countries Vol. 2: Africa* (Boulder: CO, 1988).

Dudley, B.J., *Instability and Political Order; Politics and Crisis in Nigeria* (Ibadan: 1973).

Duvenger, Maurice, *Political Parties* (New York: Wiley, 1954)

Everson, David H., *American Political Parties* (New York: New Viewpoints, 1980).

Ezera, Kalu, *Constitutional Developments in Nigeria*, 2nd ed. (Cambridge: Cambridge University Press, 1964).

Falola, Toyin and Inhonvbere, Julius, *The Rise and Fall of Nigeria's Second Republic, 1979-84* (London: 1985).

Graf, Dr. William D., *Elections 1979: The Nigerian Citizens' Guide to Parties, Politics, Leaders and Issues* (Lagos: A *Daily Times* Publication).

Grimal, Henri, *Decolonization: The British, French, Dutch and Belgian Empires, 1919-1963,* trans. Stephen De Vos (Boulder, Colorado: Westview Press, 1978).

Joseph, Chief Lai, *Nigeria's Elections: "The Bitter Truth,"* (Lagos: Nmogun Commercial Printers Limited, 1981),

Katz, Richard S., *A Theory of Parties and Electoral Systems* (Baltimore and London: The Johns Hopkins University press, 1980).

Key, V.O. *Politics, Parties and Pressure Groups, 5th ed* (New York: Cromwell, 1964).

Kirk-Greene, AHM, *Crisis and Conflict in Nigeria 1967-70,* (Oxford: Oxford University Press, 1971).

Kousoulas, D. George, *On Government and Politics, 4th ed* (North Scituate, Massachusetts: Duxbury press, 1979).

Lowell, Lawrence, *Government and Parties in Continental Europe* (Boston: 1986).

Mackintosh, John P., *Nigerian Government and Politics* (Evanston: Northwestern University Press, 1966).

Markovitz, Irving Leonard, *Power and Class in Africa: An Introduction to Change and Conflict in African Politics* (New Jersey: Prentice Hall, Inc., 1977).

Mendoza, Manuel G. and Napoli, Vince, *Systems of Society: An Introduction to Social Science, 2nd ed.* (Lexington, Massachusetts: D.C. Heath and Company, 1977).

Neustadt, Richard E., *Presidential Power: The Politics of Leadership from FDR to Carter* (New York: John Wiley and Sons, Inc., 1980).

Obasanjo, General Olusegun, *My Command: An Account of the Nigerian Civil War, 1967-1970* (London: Heineman Educational Books Ltd., 1981).

Odumosu, Oluwole Idowu, *The Nigerian Constitution: History and Development* (London: Sweet and Maxwell, 1963).

Ojiako, James O. Nigeria, *Yesterday, Today, and...* (Onitsha: Africa Educational Publishers (Nig.) Ltd., 1981).

Oyediran, Oyeleye, ed. *Survey of Nigerian Affairs, 1976-1977* (Lagos: Nigerian Institute of International Affairs, 1981).

Plano, Jack C. and Greenberg, Milton, *The American Political Dictionary*, 6th ed. (New York: Holt Rinehart and Winston, 1979).

Post, K.W.J., *The New States of West Africa*, (Great Britain: C. Nicholls and Company Ltd., 1964).

Post, K.W.J., *The Nigerian Federal Election of 1959: Politics and Administration in a Developing Political System* (Oxford: Oxford University Press, 1963).

Riker, William E., *Federalism: Origin: Operation, Significance,* (Boston and Toronto: Little, Brown and Company, 1964).

Rossiter, Clinton, *Parties and Politics in America,* (Ithaca and London: Cornell University Press, 1960).

Schwab, Peter, *Biafra,* (New York: Facts on File, Inc., 1971)

Schwarz, Frederick A.O. Jr., *Nigeria: The Tribes, The Nation, Or The Race – The Politics of Independence,* (Massachusetts: The M.I.T. Press, 1965).

Shattschneider, E.E., *Party Government* (New York: Rinehart, 1942).

Sklar, Richard L., *Nigerian Political Parties: Power In An African Nation*, (Princeton, New Jersey: Princeton University Press, 1963).

Sorauf, J. Frank, *Party Politics in America. 4th ed* (Boston: Little Brown & Company, 1980).

Tandon, Yashpal and Chandarana, Dilshad, ed., *Horizons of African Diplomacy* (Nairobi: East African Literature Bureau, 1974).

The Royal Institute of International Affairs, *Nigeria: The Political and Economic Background* (Oxford: Oxford University Press, 1960).

Federal Ministry of Information, *The Struggle for One Nigeria,* (Lagos: Federal Ministry of Information, 1976).

Whitaker Jr., C.S., *The Politics of Tradition: Continuity and Change in Northern Nigeria, 1946-1966* (New Jersey: Princeton University Press, 1970).

Woll, Peter and Binstock, Robert, *America's Political System, 3rd ed.* (New York: Random House, 1979).

ARTICLES

Adeniran, Dr Tunde, 'The Two-Party System and the Federal Political Process' (unpublished manuscript)

Akinola, Anthony. A., "Why Alliances Fail in Nigeria," *West Africa,* (8 February 1982), p. 361.

Akinola, Anthony. A., "A Critique of Nigeria's Proposed Two-Party System," *The Journal of Modern African Studies,* Vol. 27, Issue 01 (March 1989), pp. 109-123.

Akinola, Anthony. A., "Manufacturing the Two-Party System in Nigeria," *The Journal of Commonwealth and Comparative Politics,* Vol 28, Issue 3 (1990), pp. 309-327.

Awolowo, Obafemi. "Twelve Months of Independence," *The Service,* II, (Nov. 4, 1961), pp. 28-29.

Charlesworth, James C. "Is Our Two-Party System Natural?", *American Academy of Political and Social Science Annals* (1948), p. 259.

Cole, Babalola. "The Military Government of Nigeria: Preparation for Democracy," *Short Essays in Political Science,* IX (1982), pp. 1-4.

Cowell, Alan. "In Nigerian Vote, Old Leaders Come Out Fighting," *New York Times* (3 May 1982), p. A2.

Dash, Leon, "Ethnic Past of Politics Tests Nigeria," *The Washington Post* (4 March 1983), pp. A17 and A19.

Ekpu, Ray, "Waziri: Why Are Rich Men in Politics," *Sunday Times* (16 May 1982), p. 7.

Harris, Richard, "Nigeria: Crisis and Compromise", *Africa Report* (March 1965), pp. 25-31.

Iroh, Eddie. "Nigeria: Radicals in Turmoil," *Africa,* 118 (June 1981), pp. 14-17.

Joseph, Richard A. "The Ethnic Trap: Notes on the Nigerian Campaign and Elections 1978-79," *Issue,* XI, (Spring/Summer 1981), pp. 17-23.

Lipson, Leslie. "The Two-Party System in British Politics." *American Political Science Review,* 47 (1953), pp. 337-58

Mackintosh, John P. "Federalism In Nigeria," *Political Studies,* X (1962), pp. 223-47.

Okadigbo, Chuba. "Creating the New Out of the Old," *African Concord,* (London: 20 February 1986).

Osadebay, Chief Dennis. "Party Alliance: It Happened Before," *Sunday Times* (21 March 1982), pp. 13 and 15.

Oshodi, Wale, "Dilemma of Political Associations," *National Concord* (27 July 1989).

Oyediran, Oyeleye and Agbaje, Adigun, "Two-Partyism and Democratic Transition in Nigeria," *The Journal of Modern African Studies,* Vol. 29, Issue 2 (June 1991), pp. 213-235.

Oyovbaire, Sam Egite. "Can the Civilians Triumph?," *African Concord,* (12 February 1988).

Tamuno, Tekena N. "Separatist Agitations in Nigeria Since 1914," *The Journal of Modern African Studies,* 8, 4 (1970), pp. 563-84.

"The Most African Country: A Survey of Nigeria," *The Economist,* (23 January 1982).

"The Political Debate and the Struggle for Democracy in Nigeria," *Review of African Political Economy,* No. 37 (December 1986), p. 45.

Whitaker, Jr., C.S. "Second Beginnings: The New Political Framework," *Issue,* XI (Spring/Summer 1981), pp. 2-13.

OFFICIAL PUBLICATIONS

Annual Report of the Education Department, Northern Provinces (1925).

House of Representatives Parliamentary Debates (Lagos: Nov. 19, 1960).

House of Representatives Parliamentary Debates (Lagos: Nov. 29, 1960).

House of Representatives Parliamentary Debates (Lagos: Nov. 30, 1961).

The Constitution of the Federal Republic of Nigeria 1979 (Lagos: Department of Information).

NEWSPAPERS AND PERIODICALS

Africa Now (November 1982).

Daily Times (2 August 1960, 23 November 1962, 2 July 1963, 4 July, 1963, 10 July 1963, 12 November 1965, 25 April 1967, 2 May 1967, 28 May 1967, 31 July.

1975, 4 February 1976, 3 July 1979, 25 July 1979, 8 August 1979, 17 August 1979, 18 August 1979, 7 September 1979, 11 September 1979, 27 September 1979, 28 February 1982, 14 January 1983).

New African (February 1983).

West African, 19 May 1962, 2 June 1962, 9 June 1962, 27 July 1981, 17.

August 1981, 3 May 1982, 10 May 1982, 3 January 1983, 24 January 1983, 31 January 1983, 28 February 1983.

INDEX

A

Abdulfatah Ahmed 130-1
Abiola 125
AC (Action Congress) 127-8
accord 91-5, 101-2
Acknowledgements ix
ACN (Action Congress of Nigeria) 128-9
Action Congress (AC) 127-8
Action Congress of Nigeria, *see* ACN
Action Group, *see* AG
activities, political 95, 116
AD (Alliance for Democracy) 126-8
administration 2, 4, 6, 43, 67, 105-6, 114, 140
AFRC (Armed Forces Ruling Council) 113-14, 116, 118-19
Africa 6, 93, 102, 113, 138, 141-2, 144
Africa Report 60-1
African 21-2, 37, 143
African Concord 122, 142
African Elections Database 124
African Political Economy 107, 143
AG (Action Group) 11, 13-14, 21, 23, 25-7, 30-1, 33-57, 59-60, 62, 73, 96, 128
AG/UPN 87, 102-3
agents 101, 108
agitation 39, 48, 51, 69, 71
Akinola 102, 137, 141
Akinola, Anthony A. 113, 134

Akintola 50, 53, 55-7, 63
Akinyemi 133
Alhaji Dauda Adegbenro 55
Alhaji Shehu Shagari 86-7, 89, 91-2
Alhaji Waziri Ibrahim 86, 99-100
Aliyu Wamakko 130-1
All Nigeria People's Party, *see* ANPP
All Peoples Party (APP) 126-7
All Progressive Grand Alliance (APGA) 129
All Progressives Congress, *see* APC
allegations 41, 56-7, 104, 129, 134
alliance 30, 33, 35-6, 42, 57-60, 73, 88, 95-6, 100-3, 126-9, 133
political 129
Alliance for Democracy (AD) 126-8
Alliances Fail in Nigeria 102
ally 33, 36, 63, 97, 99, 106
alteration 82
Amaechi 130
amalgamation 3-4, 6-7, 15
grand 1-2
America 10, 141
American Political Parties 138
American Political Science Review 142
American politics 97
amnesty 78
Anglo-Nigeria Defense Pact 46
ANPP (All Nigeria People's Party) 111, 127-9
antagonism 27, 42, 51

Anthony 137, 141
APC (All Progressives Congress) 129-30, 132-3
APC Governor of Ekiti State 132
APGA (All Progressive Grand Alliance) 129
APP (All Peoples Party) 126-7
ar 73, 99
areas
    local government 82, 85
    minority 39, 41, 97
    non-Muslim 8-9
    war-affected 76
Arikpo 28-9, 63, 137
Armed Forces Ruling Council, see AFRC
arrangement
    political 5, 106
    tripartite 5
assets 111-12
associations 16, 81-2, 97, 108, 111-12, 115-19
Atiku 131-2
authority 2, 4, 9, 19, 29, 67, 113, 117
    obeying state 4
autonomy, regional 17, 32
Awo 14, 29, 75-6, 137-8
Awolowo 5, 14, 41, 46, 54, 57, 60, 75-6, 137-8, 142
Azikiwe 11, 13-14, 26-8, 37, 91-3, 103-4, 138

B

Babangida 116, 119-21, 124-5
Babangida Aliyu 130-1
backward North 67
    relatively 42
Baltimore 25, 51, 137, 139
ban 41, 75, 85, 110, 112-13
Berkeley and Los Angeles 15, 21, 137-8

Biafra 73, 75-8, 103, 140
Biafran troops 75-8
Biafrans 75, 77-8
Bibliography 137, 139, 141, 143
bill 49
birth 2, 5, 13, 17, 99
bodies, political 12
Bolaji 132-3
Boston 21, 122, 139-41
Boulder 21, 113, 138-9
boycott 61-2
Brigadier Ejoor 77
Britain 10, 45-6
British 1, 4-7, 9, 11, 15-16, 21, 39, 69-70, 139
British Administration 1, 3, 7, 43, 45
British administrators 7-8, 45, 71
British Government 47, 69
British officials 29
British Politics 142
Buell 8-9, 138
bureau 106, 108

C

Cambridge 14, 53, 137-8
Cambridge University Press 20, 53, 138
Cameroons 11, 25
campaigns 39-40, 60, 86-7, 142
candidates 79-81, 86, 124, 126-8, 131
capability 45, 78, 94, 99
census 59-60
centre 22-3, 32-3, 53, 120, 133
chairman 99, 109, 130-1
Change and Conflict in African Politics 6, 66, 139
Change in Northern Nigeria 141
Chapter VI 79, 81, 85
Chief Akintola 50, 52-6, 59, 63, 98
Chief Awolowo 46, 51-3, 57, 74-6, 91, 100, 103-4

Chief Awolowo's British 47
Chief Moshood Abiola 124-5
Chief Obafemi Awolowo 13, 26, 44, 86, 88, 100, 104, 128
Christian missionaries 8
Chuba Okadigbo 121-2
civil war 68, 72-3, 75-6, 78, 98
civilian rule 109-10
civilians 67-8, 85
class, political 105
co-operation 48-50, 93, 101, 106
coalition 36, 38, 40, 42-3, 46, 53, 59, 91-2, 95, 103
Col 46-7
Coleman 15, 19, 31, 137-8
colonial masters 5, 16, 30-1
colonial rule 45
Colonial Secretary 32, 37, 39
Colonialism 1, 3, 5-7, 9, 11, 13, 15, 17, 19, 21, 23, 46
colonies 2, 10, 21
commission 56, 75, 82, 109, 111, 117
committed participants 101
Company 21, 73, 139-40
comparative politics 141
compromise 60, 63, 102-3, 142
Concord 143
conferences 28, 32, 38, 70-1
conflict 6, 45, 51, 53, 66, 139
Congress for Progressive Change 128
constituencies, national 83
constitution 12, 22-3, 25, 27-9, 32, 36, 71, 79, 81-2, 85, 88, 144
 new 14, 22, 29, 32, 79, 83
 presidential 68, 79, 92
Constitutional Developments in Nigeria 53, 138
contest 34, 39, 114, 132
context 41, 49, 63, 97, 99, 134
continuity 4, 6-7, 43, 141
Continuity and Change in Northern Nigeria 4
contributions 68
control 26, 38, 40, 50, 52, 58, 60, 70
convention 28, 53, 118
 special 28, 131
cooperation 88-9
correlations 87, 126
corruption 18, 46, 57, 110, 135
counter-motion 31
country 1-2, 5-6, 11, 13, 21, 41, 71, 73-4, 97, 102, 108, 112, 117, 135
coup 65-7, 87, 106
court 28, 56-7, 83, 119
CPC 128-9
creation 39, 47-51, 54, 69-71, 97-8, 119-21
Creation of Mid-Western Region 48
crisis 29, 34, 51, 56, 58-60, 62-3, 73-4, 122, 125-6, 129, 138-9, 142
Crisis and Conflict in Nigeria 139
cultures 1, 3, 7, 15, 128

D

Daily Times 48, 50, 57, 60, 63, 67, 71, 74, 88, 91-2, 144
days 77, 81-2
decision 29, 33, 56, 65, 75, 98-9, 108, 110
defections 95, 130, 132
defunct NPC 98-9
demarcation, political 92
democracy 16, 50, 53, 62, 105, 107, 114, 126, 132, 134-5, 137, 142-3
Democracy in Developing Countries Vol 113, 138
Democratic Transition in Nigeria 143
destroy 56, 74

Developing Political System 43, 140
development ix, 1, 15, 32, 68, 72, 129, 132, 135, 140
   new political 50
Development of Modern Nigeria 25, 28-9, 63, 137
Development of Political Parties in Nigeria 10-11, 13-14, 138
Dilemma of Political Associations 143
disappointment 119
disenchantment 29-30, 65
disturbances 70
dominance 62, 126, 128
Dynamic Party 96-7

E

East 25, 27-30, 33-8, 40, 42, 48, 50, 53, 56, 58, 60-2, 67, 70-6, 98, 103
East African Literature Bureau 96, 141
Eastern 25, 28
Eastern and Western regions 72
Eastern government 72
Eastern House 28-9, 34, 37-8
Eastern Nigeria 66, 74, 77
Eastern Region 33, 48, 70, 75, 86, 97
Eastern Region of Nigeria 10, 138
Economic Background 29, 32, 36, 38, 42, 141
education 7-8, 10, 14, 18, 52, 107
   political 11
Education in Southern Nigeria 7
efforts 22, 25, 29, 57, 70-1, 75, 95, 98
Ekiti governorship election 132
election campaigns 99
election results 87
election riggers 115
elections 25-7, 38-41, 43, 48, 50, 60-3, 79-83, 85-9, 96-100, 103-4, 112, 114, 122, 124-6, 129-31
   fraudulent 128
   fresh 29
   governorship 124
   gubernatorial 87-8
   local government 114
   new 34
   parliamentary 104
   past 134
   postponed transitional 124
   run-off 88, 91
   single 87
   smooth 123
   transitional 126
electoral process 97, 121, 124
elimination 66
emergence 21, 25, 29, 59, 70, 85, 121, 129, 131
Emergence of Political Parties 10
emergency, state of 55-6
Emergent African States 7, 58, 137
eminent Nigerians 63
Emirs 8-9, 15
Emirs to Western education 8
enemy, common 30, 40, 42, 48
entice 99
entry 65, 98, 101
episode 26-7
era
   political 109
   pre-military 83, 86, 93, 97
ethnic groups 7, 18, 65-6
Ethnic Past of Politics Tests Nigeria 142
Europe 10, 139
Evans Brothers Nigeria Publishers-Limited 6
executions 65-6, 78
Eyo 37

Index

F

factions 55, 57, 102, 118, 129
factors 51, 72-3, 88
failure 6, 12, 21, 35, 51, 65, 73, 91, 93, 102-3, 105-6
FEDECO (Federal Electoral Commission's) 86, 91
Federal character of Nigeria 110
Federal coalition 53, 55, 59
Federal Constitution 32, 35
Federal Elections 34, 38, 40, 48, 52, 59, 73
Federal Electoral Commission 81-2, 86
Federal Electoral Commission's (FEDECO) 86, 91
Federal Government 36, 46, 56-7, 71-2, 77-8, 115
Federal Government coalition 58
Federal Government in Nigeria 21, 137
Federal House 40, 44, 46
Federal Ministry of Information 69, 141
Federal Parliament 49, 55
Federal Political Process 123
Federal Republic of Nigeria 79, 81, 85, 107, 144
Federal troops 75, 77
Federalim in Nigeria 47
Federalism in Nigeria 47, 142
federation 37, 44, 49, 56, 69, 72, 74-5, 80-2, 104, 116, 124
Federation of Nigeria 43, 69
fold 100, 102
formation 13, 19, 38, 43, 59, 81, 85
founders 17, 19, 128
framework 3, 143
freedom, political 11
fusion 96, 102

G

G7 130-1
General Babangida 106, 110, 121, 124-5
General Ibrahim Babangida 72, 106, 125-6
General Olusegun Obasanjo 68, 77, 79, 126, 128
geo-political zones 2, 72, 126
GNPP (Great Nigerian People's Party) 86, 88, 90, 100-1, 118
governance, political 4, 52, 106
government 7-9, 38, 40, 42, 46, 62-3, 66-7, 70, 72, 93, 95, 107, 117-20, 122-3, 139
  broad-based 62-3, 92
  broad-based national 62
  coalitional 42, 45
  constitutional 120
  local 14, 118
  national philosophy of 109, 122
  post-electoral coalition 83
Government and Parties in Continental Europe 122
Government involvement in Northern schools 9
government schools 9
Governor 37, 55, 74, 77
Governor Amaechi 130
Governor Rotimi Amaechi of Rivers State 129
governors 89, 101, 129-31
  aggrieved 131
Gowon 67, 78
Graf 85, 87, 97, 138
Great Nigerian People's Party, *see* GNPP
groups 3, 6, 10, 16-17, 68, 108, 112-13, 115
  minority 39, 71, 76

H

harmony, political 42
Harris, Richard 60-1
Hausa-Fulani domination 75, 77
Head of State 67, 70
Head of State and Government of Nigeria 66
helicopters 40
Heritage of Multipartism 3, 5, 7, 9, 11, 13, 15, 17, 19, 21, 23
HERITAGE of MULTIPARTISM 1
highlights 22, 32, 37, 55, 61
history 1, 21, 36, 99, 120, 129, 134
political 106
hoping 53-4
hostility 8, 52, 105
House 29, 31, 37, 49, 55, 60, 95, 132
House of Representatives 27, 30, 32, 36, 87, 132
House of Representatives Parliamentary Debates 143
Howard University ix

I

Ibadan 2, 5, 105, 115, 122, 137-8
Ibos 1, 3, 7, 65-6, 71, 76, 78, 97, 108
Ibos of Eastern Nigeria 12
Ideal People's Party (IPP) 111
ideological 51-2, 54
Imo 90, 98, 102-3
impartiality 114
impenetrable North 40
Imperial Treasury 2-3
imperialism 6, 16
imposition 120-1
impression 65, 67, 74, 93, 100
incompatibility, political 9
increment 52

independence 6-7, 10, 38-40, 42, 45-6, 69, 140, 142
Independent National Electoral Commission (INEC) 129
indirect rule 4-6, 9
indirect rule system 3-6, 9
INEC (Independent National Electoral Commission) 129
inform Nigerians 119
ING (Interim National Government) 125
Instability and Political Order 122, 138
Interim National Government (ING) 125
IPP (Ideal People's Party) 111
Irving Leonard Markovitz 6, 66
issue 39, 41, 48, 69, 87, 90, 100-1, 119, 134-5, 141-3

J

jail 60
James 137-8, 142
John West Publications Ltd 138
Journal of Commonwealth and Comparative Politics 141
Journal of Modern African Studies 70, 141, 143
Jr 4, 39, 48, 62, 87, 90, 100, 140, 143

K

Kaduna State 89, 112
Kalu Ezera 52-3
Kano 19, 31, 90, 126, 130, 132
Kwara 90, 130, 132

L

Labour 132
Labour Party 132-3

Labour Party in Nigeria 133
Lagos 3, 5, 26, 32-4, 36, 45-6, 61, 69-72, 74, 79, 82, 113-14, 118, 138-41, 143-4
  protectorate of 2
Lagos State United Front 96
language 1, 3, 8
law 4, 91
LC (Liberal Convention) 111, 115, 117-19
leaders 13, 23, 29, 36, 41, 46, 51-2, 82, 86, 88, 118, 128, 138
  national 26, 28, 37, 99, 131
  political 22, 86
leadership 29, 44, 53, 92, 94, 102, 110, 118, 122, 131, 134, 139
  national 30, 99, 104
Legislative Council 21-2
legislature 22, 93-5, 122
legislatures, regional 25, 49
lesson 93-4
letters 8, 28, 74
liabilities 111-12
Liberal Convention, *see* LC
liberation 77-8
Lieutenant-Colonel Ojukwu 74
Lieutenant-Governor 28-9
lifting 110, 112
local political organisations 10
loyalty ix, 7, 71, 97, 134
Lugard 4-5, 8
Lyttleton, Oliver 32-3

M

Mackintosh 53, 139, 142
Mackintosh, John P. 38, 47, 51-2, 55
MacPherson Constitution 21-2, 25, 27, 29-30
Majesty 34, 43-4
manifestos 48, 112, 117, 120
Massachusetts 39, 73, 139-40

masses 16, 60, 63, 114, 123
matter 13, 33-4, 37, 50, 58, 134-5
MBPP (Middle Belt People's Party) 20
meetings 65, 74, 78, 88, 131
members 11, 16, 21-2, 26-8, 30, 47, 49, 97, 104, 106, 111-13, 116, 121, 123, 132
membership 14, 18, 39, 82, 109, 117
merger 17, 20, 92, 103-4, 112, 132
Mid West 78
Mid-West 47-9, 58, 61-2, 66, 71-2, 74-5, 77, 97, 102
Mid-West area 60, 76
Mid-West Democratic Front 96-7
Mid-West region 50
Mid-West seats 48
Mid-West state 50, 77
Mid-Western Region 48
  new 60
Mid-Western state 53
Mid-Westerners 77
Middle Belt People's Party (MBPP) 20
Middle-Belt region 98
Middle Zone League (MZL) 21
Midwest Region 41
military 63, 65, 70-1, 73, 98, 104-5, 115, 120, 135
military administration 68, 79, 85
Military Government of Nigeria 50, 142
Military Interlude and Events of Consequence 67, 69, 71, 73, 75, 77, 79, 81, 83
ministers 27-9, 31-3, 36, 62, 99, 115
  regional 27
minorities 39, 70-2, 76, 113
mobilisation, political 40
Modern Nigeria 25, 28-9, 63, 137
monolithic North 86

motion 30-1, 37, 42
mouthpiece 14-15
Muhammadu Buhari 127-8
Multipartism 103
Musa Kwankwaso 130-1
Muslim areas 8-9
MZL (Middle Zone League) 21

N

naira 111-12
nation 10-11, 31, 39, 58, 62, 79, 87, 92-4, 107, 110, 113-15, 119, 131, 134, 140
National Concord 110, 113-17, 119
National Convention of Nigerian Citizens 96
National Council of Nigeria 11-12, 25
National Council of Nigeria and the Cameroons, *see* NCNC
National Council of Nigerian Citizens 12
National Government 38, 40, 52, 54
    cobbled-together Interim 125
National Independence Party (NIP) 29
National Party of Nigeria, *see* NPN
National Republican Convention (NRC) 119, 124-5
National Union Party (NUP) 111
nationalism 6, 15, 19, 31, 36, 138
Native Administration 16-17
native authorities 16, 21
Native Problem in Africa 7-9, 138
natural rulers 4-5, 19
nature 6, 10, 14, 21, 45, 105, 107
NCNC (National Council of Nigeria and the Cameroons) 11-12, 14, 17, 21, 23, 25-30, 33-43, 47-50, 57-9, 62, 70, 73, 87, 96, 103

NCNC Alliance 56, 59
NCNC leadership 43, 57, 60
NCNC members 30, 58
NCNC ministers 27-8
NCNC/NPP 87, 102
NEC 111-17, 120
NEC report 118-19
NEPU (Northern Elements Progressive Union) 11, 19-20, 36, 41, 96, 102
New Jersey 4, 6, 26, 66, 137, 139-41
New PDP 131
New PDP Merger Good for Nigeria 132
New Political 143
New Political Framework 87
New Political Morality 110
new states 39, 48, 69
    creation of 49, 70
New States of West Africa 8, 140
Newswatch 114, 118, 120-1, 132
NGF (Nigerian Governors' Forum) 130
NGF chairman 130
Niger 90, 131
Niger Delta Congress 96-7
Nigeria 1-3, 5-7, 10-15, 17-19, 21, 38-9, 42-5, 47-8, 67-70, 73-5, 92, 105-7, 133-5, 137-8, 140-2
    citizen of 82, 109
    dominated 95
    granted 13
    independent 15, 40
Nigeria, James O. 140
Nigeria
    left 5
    politics of 11
    republican 60
    united 78
Nigeria Focus 113
Nigeria Labour Party (NLP) 111
Nigeria Peoples 128

Index

Nigeria Peoples Party 127
Nigeria People's Welfare Party (NPWP) 111, 116, 119
Nigeria Publishers 66
Nigeria Publishers-Limited 137
Nigerian Citizens 138
Nigerian Citizens' Guide to Parties 82
Nigerian Civil 77
Nigerian Civil War 75-6, 138-9
Nigerian Constitution 1, 3, 12, 14, 18, 109, 140
Nigerian constitutionalists 134
Nigerian currency 75
Nigerian electoral management 134
Nigerian Federal Election 43, 140
Nigerian federalism 21
Nigerian Government and Politics 38, 52-3, 55, 139
Nigerian Governors' Forum (NGF) 130
Nigerian history 62
Nigerian Institute of International Affairs 140
Nigerian Labour Party 117
Nigerian leaders 69
Nigerian leadership 99
Nigerian nation 134
Nigerian National Alliance, see NNA
Nigerian National Congress, see NNC
Nigerian National Democratic Party, see NNDP
Nigerian newspapers 13
Nigerian party system 133
Nigerian People's Party, see NPP
Nigerian People's Welfare Party 113
Nigerian Political Parties 26, 28, 30, 37, 140
Nigerian politicians 89, 94
Nigerian politics 26, 41, 51, 54, 68, 79, 95, 134
annals of 40, 95
Nigerian populace 114
Nigerian population 114, 121
Nigerian Prime Minister 38
Nigerian scholar 52
Nigerian society 107, 135
Nigerian students in London 46
Nigerian territories 46
Nigerian Tribune 115
Nigerian Vote 104, 142
Nigerian workers 12
Nigerian youth 54
Nigerians 7, 10, 47, 49, 65, 72, 79, 92, 94, 105, 107-8, 115-16, 119-21, 123-4, 126
Nigeria's Elections 3, 139
Nigeria's electoral officials 134
Nigeria's heterogeneity 45
Nigeria's heterogeneous society 123
Nigeria's history 5
Nigeria's independence 46
Nigeria's multipartism 21
Nigeria's party system 9, 68
Nigeria's politics being 108
Nigeria's Vice President 93
NIP (National Independence Party) 29
NLP (Nigeria Labour Party) 111
NNA (Nigerian National Alliance) 59, 61, 95-6, 100
NNA/NPN 98
Nnamdi 138
Nnamdi Azikiwe 10, 12, 20, 26, 34, 37, 43, 62, 86-7, 104, 138
NNC (Nigerian National Congress) 111, 117-19
NNDP (Nigerian National Democratic Party) 59-60, 62-3, 96-8
North 3-4, 8-9, 12-13, 15-19, 21-2, 27, 30-1, 33-6, 38-42, 47-8, 53, 58-62, 65-7, 97-9, 125-6

North Central 2
North-Eastern 2
North Scituate 139
Northern 25, 40, 143
Northern and Southern protectorates 1
Northern descent 18
Northern domination 73
Northern Elements Progressive Union, *see* NEPU
Northern fear 42
Northern leaders 66, 70
Northern leadership 67
Northern life 18
Northern members 31
Northern Nigeria 2, 15-16, 20, 141
Northern origin struck 67
Northern Party 20
Northern People 31
Northern People's Congress, *see* NPC
Northern protectorate 2
Northern province 5
Northern Provinces 9
Northern Region 18, 72
Northern region of Nigeria 69
Northern regionalism 15, 18
Northern schools 9
Northern towns 16
Northern troops 74
Northern Western Eastern South Lagos Total Region Region 35
Northerners 13, 15, 17, 31-2, 41, 66, 78, 99
  potential nationalistic 15
Northwestern University Press 38, 52, 139
NPC (Northern People's Congress) 11, 15, 17-20, 25, 27, 31, 33, 35-6, 38-43, 45, 48-9, 58-60, 62, 83, 96-8
NPN (National Party of Nigeria) 86, 88-92, 95-103, 118, 126
NPN/NPP accord 92-3

NPP (Nigerian People's Party) 59, 86-8, 90-2, 95, 100-2, 104, 118
NPWP (Nigeria People's Welfare Party) 111, 116, 119
NRC (National Republican Convention) 119, 124-5
number 21, 34, 38, 60, 66, 85, 108-9, 111, 126, 132
NUP (National Union Party) 111

O

Obafemi 137-8, 142
Obafemi Awolowo 2, 14, 29, 46, 75, 137
Obasanjo 126, 130-1, 139
objectives 6, 11, 15, 17-18
occasions 113, 124, 128, 135
Odumosu 3, 12, 14, 18, 140
office 10, 67-8, 79, 82-3, 88, 105, 110, 112, 134, 138
office-holders, political 105
office of president 80-1
Office of President 79
Ojiako 34, 43, 51, 54, 100, 140
Olusegun Obasanjo 127, 131
opponents, political 63, 107
opposition 45-7, 123
  official 36, 38, 103
optimism 104, 119-20
organization 12-13
Oxford 43, 138-41
Oxford University Press 2, 29, 43, 139-41

P

pact 46
Parliamentary Debates 46-7
participant, active 100
participation 63, 112
  direct 22
  political 108
Participation in Politics and Elections 112

Index

parties 11-16, 18-21, 27-8, 33-42, 46-8, 50-5, 82-3, 85, 91-5, 97-104, 107-9, 111-13, 120-2, 127-33, 138-40
   aggrieved 130
   conservative 60
   defunct 87
   incumbent 122
   major 15, 20, 25, 41-2, 51, 53, 91, 101-2, 132
   minor 97, 133
   minority 97
   nucleus 96
   reform-oriented 19
   ruling 48, 118
   strong 133
   unified progressive 129
Parties and Politics in America 140
parties and precedents 113
Parties and Pressure Groups 139
parties train 107
partition 72
   uneven 73
party development, political 12
Party Development in Northern Nigeria 15
party leaders 29, 52-3, 87
party members 28, 94
party politics 77, 95, 107, 110, 116
Party Politics in America 141
Party System 27, 65, 67, 69, 71, 73, 75, 77, 79, 81, 83, 107, 133, 141
past politicians 110
Patriotic Nigerian Party (PNP) 111
Patriotic People's Party (PPP) 111
Patterns of Majoritarian and Consensus Government 133
Patterns of Majoritarian and Consensus Government in Twenty-One Countries 133
PDP (People's Democratic Party) 126-34

PDP governor of Plateau State 130
PDP leadership 130
PDP politicians defecting 132
PDP Splits 131
People's Democratic Party, see PDP
People's Front of Nigeria, see PFN
Peoples Redemption Party, see PRP
People's Solidarity Party, see PSP
perceptions 102, 118
persuasion 94
Peter 140-1
PFN (People's Front of Nigeria) 111, 117-19
planners 65-6
platforms 17, 39, 120, 128-9, 132
plebiscite 49-50
pledges 8-9
PNP (Patriotic Nigerian Party) 111
policies 6-7, 10, 29, 42, 47, 54
Political Adviser 121
political alliances, avoiding 121
political appointments 52
political arena 10
political associations 110-20, 143
   recommended 119
   various 115
political astuteness 54
   demonstrated 95
Political Bureau 107-9, 121-3
   17-member 106
political criminals 113
Political Debate 107, 143
Political Dictionary 140
political disadvantage 48
political dissatisfaction 22
political editor 117
political elites, new 45
political equation 22
political groupings 108, 118
political insincerity 58
political justice 20
political largesse, sharing 95
political loyalties 9

political models 106
Political Office Holders 110
political order 107, 122, 124, 138
   new 119
political parties 6, 10-16, 18-19, 50-1, 81, 83, 85-6, 88, 101-2, 107-10, 114-15, 119-20, 122, 128-9, 138
   banned 117-18
   broad-based 133
   disciplined 14
   establishment of 79, 83
   exclusive 97
   external 23
   formed new 126
   government-sponsored 124
   minor 88
   new 110, 119, 131
   ordered 88
   regional 12
   registered 87
   well-balanced 124
political party activities 65
political party formation 129
political problems 22
political procedures 122
political process 116, 121, 141
   unifying 79
political realignment 73
political realism 7
political realist 59
political responsibilities 13
political rhetoric 41
political scene 124
Political Science ix, 133
political sensitivity 53
political structure, new 121
political struggle 77
Political Studies 47
political support 83
political tutelage 30
political warlords 121
politicians 58, 65, 85, 100, 105, 121, 126, 132, 135
   aspiring 105
   banned 115
   civilian 105
   corrupt 106
   greed-elected 135
   new breed 124
politicisation 73
politics 29-30, 38, 43, 46, 52-3, 55, 94, 99, 107, 110, 112, 121-2, 135, 137-40, 142
   ethnic 83
   external 16
   national 58
   presidential 94
   religious 101
Politics and Crisis in Nigeria 122, 138
Politics of Independence 39, 140
Politics of Leadership 139
Politics of Tradition 4, 16, 141
population 1, 46, 48, 58, 60, 116
position 26, 36, 40, 43, 49-50, 52, 56, 69, 77, 98
post 43, 60, 140
Post-independence governments in Nigeria 70
Post-independence Party Politics 45, 47, 49, 51, 53, 55, 57, 59, 61, 63
Post-military Party Politics 85, 87, 89, 91, 93, 95, 97, 99, 101, 103
Potential Two-party System 105, 107, 109, 111, 113, 115, 117, 119, 121, 123, 125, 127, 129, 131, 133
power 22, 26, 29, 32, 34, 41, 52, 56, 66-8, 94, 106, 122, 125, 132, 139-40
   governmental 49
   political 10, 12, 124
   presidential 94, 139
Power and Class in Africa 6, 66, 139

Power and Leadership in Nigeria 122
PPA (Progressive Parties' Alliance) 102-3, 118
PPP (Patriotic People's Party) 111
Pre-Independence Party Politics 25, 27, 29, 31, 33, 35, 37, 39, 41, 43
preamble 19-20
Premier 34, 37, 40, 50, 52, 55-6, 59-61
Premiers of Northern and Eastern Nigeria 55
presidency 83, 85-7, 95, 104, 126, 128, 130, 133-5
president 17, 62, 79-81, 83, 94-5, 103, 110, 129, 134-5
President Babangida 106, 112, 114, 121
President Goodluck Jonathan 129, 131
President Shagari 93-4
presidential candidates 87-9, 91-2, 126
presidential election 87, 92, 95, 101, 104, 110, 124, 126-8
Presidential Elections in Nigeria 124
prestige 9-10, 40
Prime Minister 40, 43, 55-6, 59-60, 63, 103
Princeton University Press 4, 26, 137, 140-1
Printing Division 79
programmes 14, 51, 54, 109, 119
  economic 115
Progressive Parties Alliance 100, 118
Progressive Parties' Alliance (PPA) 102-3, 118
progressives 88-9, 100, 102, 104
provinces 4-5, 143
PRP (Peoples Redemption Party) 86, 88, 90, 100-2, 118, 126

PSP (People's Solidarity Party) 111, 114, 117-19
Punch 130, 132

R

race ix, 8, 39-41, 48, 62, 140
rank, cabinet 62
re-election 130, 134
realisation 15, 50-1, 95
realities, political 49
recommendation 44, 74, 108-9
reduction 48, 52
reelection 130
referendum 50
refusal 55, 66-7, 74
Regional Government 38
regions 5, 12, 15, 21-3, 27, 32-6, 40-1, 47-51, 57, 60-2, 86, 97-8, 103
  new 41, 49-50, 61
registration 111-12, 114-15
religion 3, 8, 18, 82, 109, 134
representation 97, 100, 108
representatives 21-2, 27, 30-2, 36, 47, 87, 94, 132
Republican parties 133
Republican Party (RP) 96, 111, 117
request 37-8
requirements 88, 91, 112-13, 117
  constitutional 49, 83, 86
resign 26, 28
resignation 28, 31
resolution 31, 49
respected Nigerian 121
respective regions 22, 40
responsibility 22-3
Review of African Political Economy 107, 143
Rich Men in Politics 142
Richard 139-40, 142
Riker, William H. 21
Rivers 90, 97, 130, 132

Rossendale Books 134, 137
Rotimi Amaechi 130-1
Royal Institute of International Affairs 29, 32, 36, 38, 42, 141
RP (Republican Party) 96, 111, 117

S

Sam Egite Oyovbaire 121-2
SAP (Structural Adjustment Programme) 115
school fees 52
scramble 83, 85
SDP (Social Democratic Party) 119, 124
seats 12, 22, 26-7, 34-6, 38, 40, 42, 48, 60-2
secede 31, 33-4, 73, 75
secession 34, 67, 71-3, 103
Second Republic 105, 118, 137-8
secretary 17, 55-6
 national 100-1, 114
Selected Commentaries 134, 137
self-government 10-11, 18, 30
self-rule 30-1, 34, 42, 45
Separatist Agitations in Nigeria 70, 143
Service 46, 142
Short Essays in Political Science 142
Short Essays in Political Science Vol 50
Sir James Robertson 43-4
Sir Tafawa Balewa 55, 59, 62, 66
situation 50, 69-70, 74, 88-9
 political 73
Sklar 28, 30, 37, 140
Social Democratic Party (SDP) 119, 124
socialism, democratic 52, 54
Sokoto 90, 130, 132
South 2, 8-9, 15, 18, 30-1, 39, 43, 47, 53, 58-9, 73, 83, 86, 125-6, 128

South-Southern geo-political zones 2
South-West region 126
South-Western geo-political zone 2
Southern Nigeria 7
 protectorate of 2
Southerners 13, 16, 30, 32, 39, 58, 134
spate 131-2
stability 69
state governors 130
State House of Assembly 87
state/region 49, 71
State Total Votes Waziri Awolowo Shagari Kano Azikiwe 90
statement 75-6, 111
states 2, 39, 41, 49, 51, 66-7, 69-72, 76-7, 80-2, 85-6, 88-91, 103-4, 116, 118, 124
 creation of 20, 68, 70-1, 97-8
 highest number of 80
status, equality of 20
strength 47, 49-50, 88, 92, 99, 126
 political 47
Structural Adjustment Programme (SAP) 115
Struggle 69, 107, 141, 143
Struggle for Democracy in Nigeria 143
struggles 10
subsection 80-1
success 4, 6, 41, 46, 124
supporters 113, 122, 124, 131
surprise 59, 89, 92, 103
Survey of Nigeria 76, 143
Survey of Nigerian Affairs 79, 140
suspicion 6-7, 9, 15-16
sympathy 57, 59, 71
system 4-6, 8, 13, 17, 109
 multi-party 108
 one-party 108
 parliamentary 83, 89, 95, 103

Index

political 89, 141
presidential 95

T

table 34-5, 42, 55, 61, 89, 126, 129
Tamuno 70, 143
Tarka 21, 98
territory, exclusive 43, 97-8
theory 12-13
    political 93
Theory of Parties and Electoral 51, 139
title 30
Tiv area of Northern Nigeria 70
tradition 4, 16-17, 66, 141
Tripartism 25
Tunde Adeniran 123
two and two parties only 122
two-party system 95, 105, 107-9, 111, 113, 115, 117, 119, 121-3, 125, 127, 129, 131-3, 135, 141
    grassroots democratic 120
    manufactured 124
Two-Party System in British Politics 142
Two-Party System in Nigeria 141

U

UMBC (United Middle Belt Congress) 11, 20-1, 96, 98
UNDP (United Nigeria Democratic Party) 111
uniqueness 20-1
unitary rule 66
United Middle Belt Congress, *see* UMBC
United Nigeria Democratic Party (UNDP) 111
United Progressive Grand Alliance, *see* UPGA
United States 68, 73, 79
units 2, 4, 74, 77, 97

political 22
Unity Party of Nigeria, *see* UPN
University of California Press 15, 21, 137-8
University Press 14, 137-8
UPGA (United Progressive Grand Alliance) 59-61, 96, 98, 100, 102
UPN (Unity Party of Nigeria) 86, 88, 90-2, 97, 100-4, 118, 128
UPP 50, 56-7, 59
usurp 18-19

V

Vanguard 131, 133
vehicles 107-8, 116
victory 38, 61-3, 78, 100
voters 50, 134-5
votes 31, 39, 49, 51, 55, 61, 79-80, 86, 88-9, 104, 127-8, 130, 133
votes cast 79-81

W

war 73, 75-8, 99
Waziri 99-100, 142
Weekend Concord 118-19
West 12, 26-7, 29, 33-6, 38-40, 42, 47-53, 55-63, 66, 70, 73-5, 103, 141
West, John 75
West Africa 8, 55-6, 93-4, 98, 102-4, 106, 110, 112-13, 120-1, 140
West African 144
West African Pilot 11, 27
West impotent 50
Western nigeria 73
Western democracy 9
Western flank 59, 97, 102
Western Government 55
Western Government funds 56
Western House 38, 55
Western House of assembly 48

Western House of Assembly 26-7
Western legislature 26, 50, 62
Western Nigeria 73
Western Region 14, 51, 56, 60, 71
Western Region and Lagos 75
Western region and Lagos States 71
Western situation 55
Western values 8
Western World 46
Westview Press 21, 139
Whitaker 4, 16, 87, 90, 100, 143
William 138, 140

winner 91-2, 98, 101
work 29, 54, 57, 100, 109, 122

Y

York 138-9
Yorubas 1, 3, 7, 53, 74-5, 97, 108, 126, 129

Z

Zaria Friendly Society 16-17

www.ingramcontent.com/pod-product-compliance
Lightning Source LLC
Chambersburg PA
CBHW021357300426
44114CB00012B/1261